THE MARBLE FAUN
OF GREY GARDENS

THE MARBLE FAUN
OF GREY GARDENS

*A Memoir of the Beales,
the Maysles Brothers, and Jacqueline Kennedy*

JERRY TORRE AND TONY MAIETTA

Introduction by Albert Maysles

Querelle Press
New York, NY

Published by Querelle Press LLC
2808 Broadway #4
New York, NY 10025

www.querellepress.com

ISBN: 978-0-9995177-0-3, paper edition
ISBN: 978-0-9995177-1-0, e-book edition

Distributed by Ingram Content Group
Printed in the United States

Cover design by Linda Kosarin/The Art Department
Typeset by Raymond Luczak

For our mothers—Helen Torre, Jane Maietta ...
and Mrs. Edith Bouvier Beale

"It's very difficult to keep the line between the past and the present ... awfully difficult."
—Edie Beale

TABLE OF CONTENTS

(Collection of the author)

INTRODUCTION

"Sometimes it takes people who are so different from normal for us to understand who we really are."
—Albert Maysles

If there is one thing that I believe, and one thing that has guided me these many years, is that life, if you remain open to it, can be an extraordinary adventure. I have known this to be true in every situation that I have come across, and I know it to be true of my good friend Jerry Torre.

When I first met Jerry all those years ago, in that dilapidated mansion on the shore of Long Island, he was taking care of those other two "extraordinary characters" whom I grew to love so very much, Mrs. Edith Beale and her daughter, Edie. Though in the film *Grey Gardens* he seems to be just a handyman who was occasionally called upon by the Beales to fix a broken step or a leaky faucet, Jerry was so much more. He was their protector; his concern and love for them and their welfare touched my brother David and I deeply, and as our time together wore on, we realized that Jerry, too, was just as remarkable as the two ladies whose life we were documenting. Here was a boy of sixteen—not more than a child, himself—looking out for them—caring for them—loving them as if they were his own mother and sister. Indeed, we came to realize, in every aspect but biology, they were.

More than that, as time went on and I got to know Jerry, I realized, too, that he lived by that same rule that my brother and I did. He said "yes" to life. No matter what challenging situation he found himself in (and believe me, there were plenty at Grey Gardens that would frighten most men twice Jerry's age), he went into the situation fully; working hard and doing the best he could until there was nothing left to be done. When I later got to know Jerry and learned of his astonishing life story, this seemed even more amazing to me. For a child who had every conceivable reason to say "no" to life—to throw in the towel of cynicism and resignation—Jerry always said "yes" to whatever life had to offer him. And usually with a smile on his face! I know this is the reason that, all these many years later, his life has surpassed even my wildest imaginings. It has truly been an astonishing life he has lived.

I am so happy that he has finally decided to put it all down in his life story, Grey Gardens and all, for the world to see. All those years ago, I remember Edie telling us, in one of her more candid moments, that Jerry "is quite an extraordinary character." Finally, with this book, the world will see how right she was.

—Albert Maysles
New York City, December 2014

PROLOGUE: NINTH AVENUE

It was years of living in New York City that taught me about change. Neighborhoods that I had walked in, lived in, and grew up in, knowing virtually every street corner and alleyway, would transform seemingly overnight into foreign territory. The Upper West Side, the Bowery, SoHo—all daunting places to venture into when I was growing up, were now among New York's most thriving and desired addresses. Generation after generation in this city have simply accepted it, adapted, and moved on with their lives. In the end, what choice do we have? But, as I got in my cab one November evening in 2005 and began cruising these familiar streets of Manhattan, I had no idea that another life change was in store. This change, however, would bring me back full circle to a time in my past to which I had long before bid goodbye. It was a moment in time that had been especially tender to me and has always loomed large in my memory. It was a part of my life that, in so many ways, made me the man I am today. Life has a way of taking on its own identity and asserting its plans onto you, changing everything you thought you knew and wanted. If you allow that to happen and simply give yourself over to it, it can not only change your destiny, but it can also take you to places that you never dreamed of in your wildest imagination.

Over the years, I had developed a lifestyle that worked well for me. I had been a New York City cab driver for twenty-five years, and I see now that on some level I chose the job for the freedom it provided me. Working at night in the city appealed to me, as the customers were less demanding and I usually found myself energized by the exciting pulse of Manhattan nightlife. It was my routine to drive through those areas of the city that intrigued me. There was the East Village, the West Village, Midtown, and Hell's Kitchen; specifically, the area in the West Forties known as "Restaurant Row" that was always a good area to cruise for a fare just before and after curtain-time on Broadway. I was an experienced cab driver who knew the industry, knew New York City, and could get along with most customers very easily. That was one of my strengths: an ability to remain calm under very stressful situations and be respectful and courteous to my customers. Given my personal history, you may say I was schooled in the ability to remain calm under stressful situations. God knows, in my lifetime, I had plenty of opportunities to perfect that skill.

The night was well underway, and I had collected enough money by this point in my shift to feel at ease. As the night moved along, business continued to be brisk and I found myself in a very pleasant mood. I cruised the east side of Ninth Avenue and approached the Film Center building near West 43rd Street. As I surveyed the vicinity near the entrance to the building, I noticed my next fare: a young woman with a tripod hailing me to stop. The light had changed, the traffic was very light, and I easily maneuvered my way to the curb. I then popped open the trunk of the cab and stepped out to offer my assistance to this young woman, who seemed delighted to have a helpful driver at her service. She was attractive with shoulder-length brown hair and looked to be in her early thirties. Setting the tripod in the trunk, I returned to the driver's seat, turned on the taxi meter, and looked through the open partition to greet my customer. It has always been my nature to begin a conversation with my customers. It allows the driver to find out the customer's destination but also allows the opportunity to make a human connection in a sometimes-inhumane city. It makes the night more interesting, too. For me, it is simple common sense to attempt to converse, and the customer can choose whether they wish to engage or not. This particular customer was very pleasant, and she smiled at me as she gave the address in the West Village where I was to take her.

As we began our trip, we made polite small talk. I had no idea that by the time we arrived at our destination, my life would be changed forever.

"May I ask," I began, "are you in the film business?"

Watching her through my rear-view mirror, her slight smile told me that she found my question amusing.

"Yes, I am," she remarked.

"I see," I continued. "I ask only because you don't see many people travelling the streets of New York with a tripod and film equipment."

"Actually, I have been filming all day. I film commercials for liquor companies."

Sensing her willingness to continue the conversation, I decided to forge ahead.

"I love movies," I said, feeling suddenly embarrassed at the statement. Have you ever met anyone who didn't love movies? I tried to expand on the statement. "I mean, everyone loves movies, right?"

"I guess so," she offered. "I don't really work in movies, mostly television. Although I have a few friends who work in films. Documentaries, mostly."

Ah! Something we had in common, I thought, so, I took a leap of faith. "Have you had ever seen a film called *Grey Gardens*?"

"Yes, I have," she said, apparently intrigued by my sudden reference to a thirty-year-old documentary movie. "I am very familiar with the film."

Encouraged, I went on. "Well, I am the young guy in that documentary. I'm the caretaker of the house. Of course, it has been many years since, but I find it a real treat that you know of the movie."

There was a long silence in the cab.

"Wait a minute," she said slowly and in a low voice that made me look back at her in the mirror. "You're Jerry?"

"Yes," I answered.

She leaned forward and said excitedly, "You need to contact Al Maysles. He is a friend of mine, and I have been working with him for some time now. You need to contact him—he has been looking for you for years!"

Suddenly my heart began to race. Albert Maysles was looking for *me?* David and Albert Maysles, the filmmakers who made *Grey Gardens*, were my friends from the mid-1970s when we first met, yet I had not seen them in the many years since the movie was released. It felt like an entire lifetime ago, and I only thought about that time occasionally as one does with distant, hazy memory of youthful days long gone. But this remark, that Albert was *looking* for me, made it seem suddenly immediate.

"How are they doing?" I asked, stunned by the serendipity of the situation.

She suddenly seemed pensive and hesitant, pausing for a bit before she continued. "Oh, David passed away some time ago."

That news was a blow. Passed away. How was that possible? In my mind, we were all strong and healthy young men. David had been my first friend while filming *Grey Gardens*. I guess he sensed my uneasiness at the sudden appearance of himself and his brother and their ever-present camera in the Beale's home, and he wanted to make me feel comfortable. Right off the bat, he asked for my assistance in running electric wiring to the few working outlets in the house, negotiating the various "traps" in the mansion. This simple gesture made me feel a part of the endeavor and immediately put me at ease. I began to look on him as a brother, and despite the fact that we had lost contact over the years, this news that he was dead was a shock.

My passenger reached in her bag and pulled out a business card and a pen. "Here is the phone number to the Maysles Institute," she said, writing it down on the card and then handing it to me. "You need to call them tomorrow. Albert will be thrilled to hear from you!"

I took the card from her and before I knew it, we were at her destination. I popped my trunk again, got out of the cab, and helped her to the curb with her tripod. Still somewhat overwhelmed by the sudden turn of events, I said good evening, got back in my cab, and drove away.

To say it was a very special meeting would be putting it mildly. Fate had once again entered my life, and I drove away feeling shaken to my core. The last time I had felt this way was some thirty-five years earlier, when fate had brought me to the front porch of a dilapidated mansion in East Hampton, New York. And, as had happened all those years before, I knew that something monumental was about to happen in my life.

The following afternoon, I called the Maysles Institute. A woman answered and then asked me to hold the line. There was the briefest silence before a voice came on the line that melted my heart. It was Albert Maysles. Hearing the long-lost yet still familiar cadence of his Boston accent,

I laughed with delight. We chatted briefly, each of us in disbelief that we were back in communication again, and made an appointment to get together the next day. I hung up and became over taken with emotion. After all these years, I was going to see my old friend.

That next afternoon, I drove my cab from Queens into Manhattan and turned north on 8th Avenue toward West 54th Street, the location of the Maysles Film Institute. Navigating through rush hour traffic, I approached the address searching for my friend ... and for a place to pull over. Just ahead of me, I saw a film crew assembled on the sidewalk. For a brief moment, I felt frustration, as I feared the intrusion of some film crew on location for some Hollywood movie would prevent me from my reunion. Then, standing in front of a crowd of people, I saw him ... and I realized that the film crew was there for *me!* I laughed to myself at his uncanny filmmaker instinct; of course, he was going to film our reunion. He was Albert Maysles!

So, there he was, standing on the street—searching for me, too—when his eyes met mine. I could feel the tears begin to well up inside me. I left my cab idling in the street as I approached him and opened my arms to a warm embrace. It was as if we were comrades in arms, reunited in the joy of the memories that only we two shared. Of all the people from our Grey Gardens days, only he and I remained. We were the "sole survivors" of extraordinary days spent in a magical mansion. The memories of those days had been isolated in my heart for over three decades, and now, with the embrace of this man who shared them with me, I could feel the years of stored up emotion release.

After our greeting, Albert, camera in hand, got in the passenger seat next to me with a man carrying sound equipment climbing into the back. As I glanced at the soundman in the backseat, a sadness hit me and for a moment as I thought of David Maysles. How I wished he was with us now, tucked in the back seat holding his boom mike over our heads; it would have made our reunion complete. But still, I felt that being with Albert was wonderful enough. As we stopped at a traffic light, I looked over at him; his familiar face had grown older. His hair was completely white, and his face was framed in large black glasses. But behind those glasses were his eyes—the eyes that were the "filter" for his camera. What his eyes saw, his camera saw, and eventually the whole world saw. As I looked at him, he gave me a sweet smile. It had been years since we had seen each other, but it seemed as if no time had passed at all. Suddenly, the voices of that distant summer began to echo in my mind; Edie, Mrs. Beale, David, Albert calling me away from this cold November afternoon and into the balmy days of my youth. The traffic light soon turned green and Albert and I began our journey not only through the streets of Manhattan, but back in time to the golden shores of Long Island Sound and one unforgettable summer when I was seventeen years old.

CHAPTER ONE: LIFE IN ANOTHER GARDEN

In 1964, New York City hosted the World's Fair, and my mother took me there many times. It was in the Flushing Meadows area of Queens, a short subway ride from my home in Brooklyn. I remember the subway cars with rattan seats and low, slow-moving fans, and then once outside, the tall, silver sphere that towered above as you entered the fairground. But mostly I recall the excitement of visiting strange new worlds that had seemed to appear magically from thin air—right there in my own backyard. Even the buildings that housed each unusual and exotic world were special: they were called "pavilions," and they were arranged such that you would walk through one after the other and be entertained by what each sponsor had on exhibit. One of these buildings, the Sinclair Pavilion, had dinosaurs that moved with the touch of a button. However, the pavilion I remember most clearly, and the one that had a dramatic impact on me, was the Vatican Pavilion because it housed art.

I had somehow known, without understanding why, that art—specifically sculpture—would be a part of my life. I had always been drawn to the gothic headstones that graced the gravesites at Greenwood Cemetery in Brooklyn, and it was from these massive monuments that I would find my first interest in stone sculpture. Yet it was the Vatican Pavilion at the 1964 World's Fair that really brought it into my consciousness and a lit a spark that years later became a fire of passion. Here, the beauty of "The Pieta" was explained to me by my mother, who, while grasping my hand tightly to hers, whispered, "This is the mother of Jesus looking at her son." The face of the Madonna as she looked down upon her dead son struck me; I couldn't understand how stone could reveal such tender human expression. And although it would be many years before I would pick up chisel and hammer and confront an unformed slab of stone, I guess you can say that attempting to chisel tenderness out of hard and impenetrable material has been, in many respects, the story of my life.

In order to explain where it all began, I need to begin in Brooklyn. It was our city within a city—within a city. Kensington was an Italian neighborhood that existed between a park and a cemetery. Most neighborhoods were a few city blocks; mine was limited to East 3rd Street. To the east was Greenwood Cemetery, and in my childhood world of asphalt and concrete, this was our own private green space to play in during the "dog days" of summer. The fence surrounding the cemetery had rusted after years of neglect and several of the widest gaps in the fence were known to the kids in the neighborhood. Slipping through these bowed portals, I entered the first of many "gardens" that would play such integral parts in my life. To our west was Prospect Park, where we went sled riding during the New York winters. The hill that only the most daring of us would attempt to conquer with our battered Radio Flyers was aptly named "Three Devil Hill," and one cold winter day when I attempted the feat, I struck a tree head on and tore open the bridge in my nose. It was my mother's reaction to my injury, not the injury itself, that I remember to this day: her loving concern and sweetness while tending to my wound. And it was my mother who, not long after this snowfall, I had to leave at a young age to escape my father. I yearned for the love of my mother, but she was as helpless as I was when confronted by the heavy hand of my father. Having nowhere in my home to turn, I ran as far and as fast from it as possible. It was only the strength in my body and my belief that there had to be a better life for me somewhere else that saved me.

Brooklyn had its own magic for me, or perhaps more correctly, I found a magic within myself there. I had what would best be termed a "colorful" Italian family, all of whom were devoted to our family parish, the Immaculate Heart of Mary. Our lives were centered around the church, and the standards that we lived by were dictated by its rules and regulations. My father and mother were married in this church as were all eight of my aunts from my mother's side of the family. My brothers Albert,

Anthony Jr., Robert, and I all went to parochial school there. I recall one afternoon in parochial school when our Mother Superior, Sister Aquanita, entered our classroom. Mother Superior was a commanding and intimidating presence. She stood in front of the room and slowly addressed the class. "Kneel beside your desks and pray," she said. "The President has been shot, and you all must pray for him." I don't remember registering shock or any real understanding of the situation; we simply did as we were told. I would never have imagined that, in only a few years, the boy who knelt praying for a slain president would not only come to know the family he was praying for, but that two members of that family would become the most important people in his life.

Unlike the Kennedys, my family never rose above working class. My father, Anthony, worked for the Sanitation Department in the city, and his back-breaking labor had allowed him to buy our modest home on the same block as the rest of his family. We were all within "shouting distance" of each other you might say. My grandmother's house was just doors away and very Old World, as were some other relative's homes. In my earliest years, these homes were usually where I found refuge from my father; I felt safe there—and for a short time, I was safe. His fury seemed to seethe constantly just below the surface and could erupt like a volcano at the slightest provocation. His beatings on my oldest brother, Albert, were merciless. Albert was a natural rebel; he had an untamed energy and was forever getting into trouble. With each disobedience, my father's beatings grew more savage, but they only seemed to ignite Albert's rebellion further. By the time he was a teenager, Albert was an unrepentant criminal, committing crimes of increasing degrees of severity. Strangely, my father's solution to prevent his remaining sons from turning into delinquents was to beat us even more viciously. My mother, however, was the worst victim of my father's abuse. A slight woman of little more than five feet, he would often shove her against a wall in his rage. I have imagined what my mother must have felt all the years that I was unable to protect her, and for that matter, show her the very love I know we both needed. We were living in a war zone; always on our guard for the next attack. My grandmother's house was one of the few places where I could leave my fear behind.

My grandmother had eight daughters and one son living under the same roof. The son, who was called "Rubinoff," lost his sight in World War II and never left the confines of the house. I remember him sitting next to the refrigerator for what seemed like an eternity, tuning his radio. Also living in my grandmother's house was my Aunt Virginia's husband, Benny, a wise and loving man to whom I felt very close. He worked for the New York City Transit Authority and he passed on to me a love of coin collecting, card games, and a sense of pride in my heritage. Only a few houses down the street was my Uncle Gasper. He was a kind and patient man who reveled in the simplest pleasures of life. Each autumn, he would purchase crates of Concord grapes that he would use

THE MARBLE FAUN OF GREY GARDENS

to make his own wine. I recall watching the press as it spiraled downward, pressed into the grapes, followed by the outpouring of the juice. What a rich fragrance! He would then store the freshly pressed grapes in the cellar, only feet from where he slept every night. Like the rest of my family, he had a stubborn and singular nature: very colorful, very determined, and *very* "Brooklyn." Today, I see that my background, with idiosyncratic characters such as my Uncle Gasper was somehow preparation for the even more distinct and extraordinary characters I would encounter with the Beales. Eccentricity was not something startling or frightening to me; I had grown up around it and to me it was a normal part of life.

We played the games it seemed that all city kids played. The streets were our playground, and anything that we could grasp in our hands became a toy. The kids in my neighborhood were tough, proud, and ready for a fight at the drop of a hat. My street, East 3rd, was almost entirely Italian; a few blocks away, the neighborhood was almost entirely of Irish descent. In order to maintain control over our "territory," we formed a gang, as did the boys in the other neighborhoods. When conflicts arose between the Italian gang and the Irish gang, all hell would break loose. The conflicts between our two gangs were frequent and violent, although I also remember times when we would join forces to attack another group that was threatening our "turf." It really was like *West Side Story*—but Brooklyn-style.

As we got older, and testosterone began flooding our

bodies, the conflicts between each other became stronger and more intense, as did the conflicts *within* me. I couldn't quite understand why, but, during my occasional tussles with other boys, there was an added edge of excitement that was something other than adrenaline. This culminated in an episode with a friend, when an innocent episode of wrestling and horseplay between us developed suddenly into a more serious feeling. To my friend, it may have just been more rough house play. I knew it was different for me; I could feel something stirring inside me that both scared and excited me. The feeling of being physical with a man: the rough and tender—hard and soft, push and pull—was an unforgettable sensation. I quickly pulled away from him and ran home, afraid that perhaps my erection had given me away. These feelings were doubly troubling for me, coming from the background that I did, because it was pounded into our heads by the nuns of the Catholic school that merely indulging in such thoughts was a sin that would leave us burning in Hell. So, at church the next day, I said three "Hail Marys" and four "Our Fathers" in a desperate appeal for absolution. But even then, kneeling at the altar, I glanced up at the figure of Christ nailed to the cross, and the sight of his lean, muscular arms and tight stomach would lead me to brand new thoughts and the feelings started all over again. I was actually sinning in the process of doing penance for my sins! In my childlike mind, it seemed an unending cycle that would doom me for eternity.

To be fair, however, I must confess that I had been

aware of sex for a long time. While most children develop sexual awareness in their own natural time, other children, unfortunately, have that awareness brought to them. This was the case with me. My sexual "education" had begun a few years before, and I had been "schooled" by a much older neighbor.

It first happened on Easter Sunday when I was nine years old. We all were dressed in brand new clothes that we had worn to church that morning. I had on a stiff white shirt with my first real tie that had been secured by my brothers into a double Windsor knot. We had just eaten our big Easter meal, and we joined the rest of the neighborhood congregating outside; the adults to converse on the stoops and the children to play in the street. Included in the group was an older boy who lived nearby. I don't remember his age at the time—perhaps fourteen or fifteen—but I do remember that he was old enough to smoke cigarettes in front of his parents without fear of reprimand. In fact, he boasted that he smoked his Marlboros right at the kitchen table. He was standing off to the side, smoking, while we children played together. When the others were not looking, he motioned to me to follow him as he walked away. I did so, and he led me toward a factory just down the street. Being Easter Sunday, it was closed and the trucks that were used to make deliveries were parked, unattended, in front of the factory. They were cargo trucks used to deliver baked goods, and they had large panel doors on the side that slid open to access the cavernous rear area. I watched my neighbor as he approached one of the trucks. When he got to the side door, he grasped the handle, and pulled it, and the door easily slid open. He looked back at me and then quickly ducked inside. I was confused for a moment but also curious. And something else as well; a strange churning in the pit of my stomach that was a mixture of excitement and fear. Looking back, I think I knew what was going to happen in that truck ... and something powerful inside me compelled me onward.

This began my sexual "education" at the hands of my older neighbor that continued for many years afterward. Though I was only nine years old, this was clearly not an issue to my perpetrator, who grew from adolescence to adulthood in the years of our involvement. As happens with most victims of sexual abuse, the experience was made doubly damning because, as I grew older and my hormones became active, I began to find some enjoyment in the experience. We would have sex frequently and sometimes dangerously, which also lent to the excitement of the experience. Often, we would skip school and spend the afternoon having sex in nearby Prospect Park, keeping a careful eye on the time so as to arrive home at the normal, expected hour.

As the 1960s wore on, the social and civil unrest that gripped the nation played out daily on the streets of my neighborhood. As for me, my own gang experiences were quickly turning from mischievous pranks to outright criminal activity, including instances of vandalism and petty theft. The city seemed to be under siege and our neighborhood, Kensington, was becoming a very dangerous place to live. In a vain attempt to protect their children from further harm, my parents moved us out of the city and into the "safety" of the suburbs—Holbrook, New York, right in the center of Long Island. Though many city kids would have protested the uprooting of their lives, I welcomed the change of environment as Holbrook was an area I knew well and loved. My Uncle Freddy had been constructing a country house not far from where my parents had settled us, and I had been visiting the site of his construction for years. In fact, it was very often a place of refuge for me from my father's beatings. It was here that I learned about building and gardening, and it was also here that I found refuge and consolation in the reassuring sights and sounds of nature; the fields of vegetables, the singing of crickets at night, the rush of wind through the trees above me. Somehow, they all made me feel less alone and more comforted. Years before, he had planted vegetables on the property, and near the vegetable patch was a wooden pen holding cottontail rabbits. Being a kid from the streets of Brooklyn, I was so entranced by these rabbits that I would wait for them to appear and hop into the vegetable patch. There were also pear trees whose shade would protect the many box turtles that wandered about freely. In Holbrook, we were living just a few miles from this wonderful place. I was very happy.

Unfortunately, this blissful period was not to last long, as my mother grew increasingly unhappy with our new surroundings and the distance from her family in Brooklyn. After only a year in the country, my parents packed us up and moved us back into the city. Not back to Brooklyn, since by this time our old neighborhood had become something resembling a war zone, but to a sedate neighborhood in Queens.

The relative tranquility of our new surroundings did not rub off on my father, however, and his beatings took on an even more brutal nature. The only difference was now I was a teenager, which seemed, for some reason, to make him even angrier at me. Perhaps it was the threat of my approaching manhood, with the corresponding approach of his middle age, that angered him. Was I a constant reminder that his youth and his best years were behind him? Or was it his snowballing alcoholism? Whatever the reason, his behavior was increasingly out of control. Though I had to say goodbye to my garden and hens when we moved to Queens, I was able to bring my rabbits along with me. For some reason, my love for nature inspired a seething contempt in my father, and one day when I returned home from school I discovered that he had slaughtered them all. I was beside myself with grief and rage over this senseless act of cruelty. Somehow, I had grown to tolerate his viciousness toward me, but his violence against defenseless creatures was a turning point and I decided that I had to leave.

I was fourteen the first time I ran away from home. My destination was my uncle's farm near Holbrook, but before reaching it, I was picked up by the local policeman for being a minor. I knew this policeman from our family's brief residence in the area; his name was Stephen Kalbacker and he was the father of one of my classmates in Holbrook. I pleaded with him to let me go, but because of my age, he really had no choice but to return me to my father's home. But a seed had been planted. After that initial attempt, my eventual escape from Queens was a foregone conclusion for me.

The final straw occurred eighteen months later, when I was accepted into the State University of New York (SUNY) at Cobleskill, about 165 miles north of New York City. Despite having accomplished a major achievement of obtaining early acceptance into college, my father inconceivably refused to allow me to attend. That did it. I would no longer allow this monster to dictate what I could and could not do with my life. I was old enough to know that I could survive on my own, away from the insanity of this situation, so I packed my bags and I set off for Long Island once again. This time, however, I did not return home. I arrived in Holbrook where I sought the help of Mr. Kalbacher—the very same man who returned me to my father all those months before. Now, fully aware of the situation I was facing at home, he did not return me to my father. I was allowed to stay with the Kalbacker family on the stipulation that I complete my high school education and graduate. I was delighted and immediately enrolled myself back in Sachem High School to complete my studies.

After my graduation, I was at a loss as to just what to

do with my young life. Returning to my family in Queens was not an option, nor was enrolling at SUNY Cobleskill since, without my father's financial assistance, paying the tuition was far out of my reach. Once again, Mr. Kalbacker came to my rescue. He had a fishing cottage outside of Holbrook on the shores of Long Island sound, and offered me the opportunity to live there—rent free—but with the condition that I find a job to support myself as soon as possible. He needn't have told me twice. Living on my own? Rent free? On the shore? I was packed before he finished making the offer.

In looking for employment, I wanted a job that was outdoors, working with the earth and soil and nature that had so often served as a safe haven for me in my turbulent adolescence. And God knows I was in the perfect area to look for such a job. The eastern shore of Long Island is dotted with one palatial home after another; each property lusher than the next, and all of them requiring staffs of gardeners and groundskeepers. The villages of Sagaponack, Bridgehampton, Amagansett, and East Hampton were all within a few miles of each other and of me.

One day I was looking through the classifieds of an East Hampton newspaper when I saw an ad for an assistant gardener needed on an estate. I answered the ad, and before I knew it I was interviewing for the job with a severe, no-nonsense woman name Charlotte, who managed the household staff. I was told it was the home of the famous industrialist Gerald Geddes; well, famous to everyone but me, as I had never heard of him. Perhaps it was this indifference to his stature coupled with my enthusiasm that impressed Charlotte enough to offer me the job. I was thrilled. Not only would I be working on one of the most exquisite grounds in the one of the most beautiful areas of the country, I would be paid $100 per week for the privilege. And, lodging was included in the job—I would have my very own room on the grounds of the estate! I accepted the position on the spot, rushed back to the fishing cabin, gathered up what few possessions I had, and moved into my new home. In just a few years, I had gone from the warzone of Kensington to residing in one the toniest zip codes in all of the United States: East Hampton, New York.

True, I was only a hired hand, but that didn't matter to me. For the princely salary I was paid, I was required to do very little. I was to mow the great lawns and tend to the gardens, clean the pool, and make sure that all of Mr. Geddes's cars had full tanks of gas always. For someone who loved nature and its wonders, I was in heaven. I performed the tasks of my job with ease. But the most challenging part of the job for me—and one of the most crucial—was to remain "invisible" while performing them. It was an absolute law on the estate that at no time was I ever to be "seen" by Mr. Geddes, any member of his family, or any of their guests. I confess, when I was first told of this—from the great man himself on my first day of work—I snickered a bit. How was I to mow and rake the acres of lawn, clean the pool, trim, seed, and water the gardens and maintain the operation of his fleet of vehicles without ever being seen? I posed this question to him during our interview. His response: "That's your problem."

It was the first—and last—time I ever made eye contact with the man.

This request to "not be seen and not be heard" (and which I later discovered was pretty much compulsory at most great Hampton estates) didn't bother me. I quickly nodded my head in agreement, although I admit to many close calls over the ensuing years. I would be working away in the yard, raking the lawn or tending the flower beds, and I would suddenly hear the crunch of gravel under the car tires of my employer. I would then have to drop whatever I was doing, and whatever tool I was using at the time, and make a running dive for the nearest bush, often making it inside its camouflage of shadow just in time. It was a scene worthy of a Buster Keaton comedy.

Tending to the plants in the vast gardens of the estate and interacting with wildlife that I came upon had a healing effect on my soul; the simplicity and sheer majesty of nature as it unfolded before my eyes, unencumbered by interference of human beings, was a revelation. Nature was so simple; it just did what it was designed to do without pretense or hidden motivations. Something about its divine simplicity spoke deeply to me. Plus, the ability to support myself was empowering beyond belief. I no longer had to rely on a madman to supply me with my basic needs; I could do it on my own.

Within a few weeks, I had saved up enough to buy a
ten-speed bicycle, which allowed me to leave the confines
of the estate and begin to explore the area around me. With
each excursion outside of the estate, I would grow bolder
and bolder and go out farther and farther into the village
of East Hampton. I loved biking through the village and
its narrow roads, its small shops and storefronts giving
the appearance of a small, welcoming New England town.
Mostly, however, I was drawn to the quiet beach access
roads on the edge of the village.

One day I was drawn away from the Geddes's estate
toward the water and to the fairly secluded area known
as Georgica Pond. There was a soft green lawn in the
distance that fairly invited me to lay down and take a
quiet nap. So, I parked my bike and stretched out in the
shade of a copper beach tree. I laid back, propping myself
up against its enormous trunk, and was just about to close
my eyes when I saw something emerging from the tree
line in the distance. At first, I couldn't make out what I
was looking at, and then I discerned that it was two peaks
of a roof that seemed to rise up out of the forest of trees.
I had never noticed these peaks before, even though I had
biked through the area on several occasions. Something
about this roof made me curious. It truly looked as if it
had sprung up out of the trees that were surrounding
it, and I had to see what more there was to this strange
sight. I proceeded to get back on my bicycle and rode in
the direction of the peaks of the roof. I headed down Lily
Pond Lane, following it as it curved around the pond and

came to an end at the intersection of Apaquogue and West End Roads.

I was stunned by what appeared before me. There, barely visible behind a thick entanglement of trees, bushes, and vines, seemed to be a house. And not just a house; even from the street I could tell that this was a mansion. Its central entranceway was bordered by a long, deep porch, framed on both sides by two large, three-storied sections that were nearly obliterated by the overgrown vines that covered every inch and seemed to suffocate the building. Ropes of bittersweet hanging from a pair of twisted catalpa trees skittered down from the house and past a car that was sitting, abandoned, in a sea of tall grass. The car must have been there for quite some time, as saplings had grown up in front and behind it; but the door looked as if it were open slightly waiting for someone to climb inside and drive off. In fact, as I walked closer toward the car, I noticed there were keys in the ignition. It was hard to tell what model of car it was (a Cadillac? Duesenberg?) or even the approximate year it had been manufactured. It looked to be from the 1930s, with its elegant low-slung curves that had lost their luster after years of exposure to the elements. Inside the car, it appeared that generations of animals had nested inside its once grand upholstery.

Who in the world did this car belong to? And what in the world was it doing here, in this tangled, twisted mass of shrubs, tree limbs, and undergrowth? It was as if I had stumbled upon an oasis, but in reverse. In this small plot of land, nature was rebelling and overtaking everything that was in her path. I looked up toward the house. If the car was abandoned, I wondered, was the house as well? How could anyone live in such a ramshackle place, especially here in wealthy East Hampton? The incongruity of what was before me was mind boggling.

I could feel my heart beat faster inside my chest as I turned away from the car and toward the house. The front door was just feet away from me. I could see the leaded glass inlay, cut in diagonal shapes, in the windows on the portico, and my curiosity was really beginning to get the better of me. I started toward the porch, but then I stopped. I was a kid of sixteen and I had no idea who—or what—if anything called this property home. It was such an unmitigated wreck of a place; with its weather-beaten shingles, dark and shuttered windows covered with vegetation, it resembled the definitive haunted house of all times. And yet, there was something more. Something intriguing—seductive. Something that was calling out to me to come closer. But I couldn't. I suddenly felt a rush of adrenaline—and fear—and I hopped back on my bike and pedaled away. I decided I would not go up to the house that day. I would wait. I would come back.

But that night, I couldn't sleep. I kept thinking about the house and the craziness of the whole situation. East Hampton had dozens of beautiful estates, homes that looked like pages right out of *Town and Country* magazine. Gorgeous estates with manicured grounds, the surf caressing nearby Georgica Beach. Suddenly, I felt the urge to go back to the house and make sure that what I had seen had indeed been real. I impulsively jumped out of bed, threw on my shorts and was out the door.

Soon, I was travelling down the same path I had been on that afternoon. As I approached the park where I had first seen the peaks of the house, I stopped. What was I doing? If I couldn't face going up to the porch in the bright sunlight of afternoon, did I really think I could muster the courage to do so in the dead of night? I was about to turn my bike around to head back to the Geddes estate, but before I did, I looked up. I could see the peaks of the mansion again against the twinkling night sky. It *had* been real! Emboldened, I got back on my bike and pedaled toward the haunted house.

Finding it in the dark was difficult because there were no street lamps and only the moon lit the way. But not for long, because as I approached the location I could see dim lights in the distance growing brighter as I drew nearer the house. A porch light was on! Not only that, I could see a light in an upstairs window near the rear of the mansion. Someone *did* live there! That was all I needed to know. I vowed right then and there that tomorrow I would knock on the door. "Tomorrow, Jerry," I said to myself as I pedaled furiously down the street toward home. "Tomorrow you're going to go to that house and introduce yourself. Come what may."

The following day I ticked off my chores as quickly as I could, energized by the thought that I was going to do something so daring. I don't know why, but I felt this compulsion to find out just who could be living in such a dilapidated state. I was fascinated, and it must have been the fascination that compelled me to do what in retrospect seems like a foolish and possibly even dangerous gesture. After all, I had no idea what I would encounter stepping onto that porch. In fact, I would be trespassing and someone might even phone the police. Such thoughts didn't occur to me then, though. I was feeling much too exhilarated by the excitement of this new adventure.

Before I knew it, my chores were done and it was time to go. I jumped on my bicycle and pedaled excitedly down the road—the sudden rush of adrenaline giving me almost superhuman energy. But as I once again approached the house, I began to question myself again. Could I go through with this? Would I really have to courage to go and knock on the door and see what was inside? I laid my bike down on the lawn and slowly approached the front porch, making my way up the stairs and onto the landing. There was a beaten-up screen door, and behind it was a large, imposing wooden "Dutch" door. I slowly opened the screen door, which made a slight wheezing noise as its hinges rotated. I was about to knock, but before I did, I peered through one of the diamond-shaped windows that encased the door. Holy Christmas! I couldn't believe it. The place wasn't empty but fully furnished! I saw chairs, sofas, drapes, sculptures, vases, paintings—all covered with cobwebs and dust. The cobwebs ran from banister to chandelier to chair to floor. Every surface I could see was covered with cobwebs … and those cobwebs were, in turn, covered with dust so that they looked like dull, grey icicles hanging down. It appeared as if no one had been inside the house for the past one hundred years! What was more, all around the room—on the floor, tables, chairs, benches, stairs—were what looked like cat food cans, piled so high that you couldn't see over them. Opposite to the door where I was standing there was a staircase that went up about five steps, turned at a right angle and rose another five or six steps, then turned again at a right angle and went up and over the foyer. There seemed to be a narrow path created on the stairs between the dirt and debris that led straight down the steps to the front door, with two other paths branching out at the foot of the stairs: one going left and one going right, and then disappearing behind piles of cans and bottles.

I was confounded by the sight. I felt as if I were in a movie because it all seemed so far removed from reality. I tried to gather my thoughts and focus on the task at hand. I was going to knock when suddenly a figure appeared at the top of the stairs. It looked like a woman, and she seemed to float down the stairs, through the cobwebs, like some sort of strange goddess descending to earth. For a moment, I felt the impulse to run, fearful that this specter may lash out at me for trespassing on her property. My heart began pounding harder as she approached. I couldn't really tell how young or old she was—her appearance was so unusual that it made guessing her age impossible. I could now see her face as she unlocked the door and slowly opened it. She had almost a child's face, with a smooth and unlined complexion. She was wearing around her body what looked like a cloth shower curtain with a floral print, and tied at the waist with what…a sweater? I could see that she was wearing torn fishnet stockings with white high-heeled pumps on her feet, and on the top of her head she wore a white chef's apron wrapped around and tied in the back with a knot.

I stood there, motionless and silent for a few moments, just staring at this exotic creature standing in front of me, not knowing if I should stay or run. Though she looked startling to say the least, there was nothing unfriendly about her demeanor. Actually, there was a tranquility in her face—a calmness that made it quite lovely. She held my gaze for a moment before a smile began to form on her lips. I was about to say "hello" when suddenly she reached out toward me—not to shake my hand but to touch the side of my face. I stood there frozen, unable to speak or move.

"Well, for goodness sake," she said in a soft voice as she stroked my hair. "The Marble Faun is here."

CHAPTER TWO: ENTERING THE GARDEN

In my tight little quarters at the Geddes estate, I had a single bed next to a window with a simple curtain and shade. Often at night I would lie very still and, depending on the cycle of the tides, I would hear the roar of the ocean and the pound of the waves breaking onto the nearby beach. This was certainly the case the night before I was to return to the mansion. Not that I would have been able to sleep anyway, as my mind was racing. I couldn't wait for 9:00 to come. That was the time that the woman wearing the shower curtain had told me I was to return to "meet Mother."

When we met earlier, I told her of my job at the Geddes estate and asked if perhaps I could help them clear away some of the brush that choked the house. I wasn't looking for money, I just wanted to help. She thought this was a good idea, but that we would have to discuss it with her mother who was resting at the moment. I should come back, she told me, the next morning and we three could meet and discuss it. I agreed, and the appointment was set.

Lying in bed, the hours were moving so slowly. Despite my restlessness, I managed to grab a few hours' sleep before I began my work on the estate that morning. As soon as my chores were completed, I took a quick shower and dressed for my appointment. I pulled out a clean sweatshirt that I had received during my days as a newspaper carrier for *Newsday*; I thought it was professional looking (after all, I had been named "Master Carrier"). I got back on my bike and headed for he estate, retracing my route from the day before.

Once I arrived, I set down my bicycle on the lawn, concealing it amongst the deep set of saplings that engulfed the area of yard near the old abandoned car. I proceeded slowly to the front porch—my nerves on fire—with a mixture of apprehension and anticipation. Standing at the front door, I knocked on the glass. As soon as I did, I saw a pair of feet hurrying down the stairs. The door swung open and there was the woman from the day before.

"Oh," she said, sounding surprised, "the Marble Faun is back."

There was that name again. I had no idea what she meant; who was this "Marble Faun" she referred to? In my enthusiasm, I blurted out, "Hello, again. It's nice to see you."

She didn't respond. She just stood there, smiling that

same vague smile as the day before. Had what I just said even registered with her? I couldn't tell. I was worried that perhaps she had forgotten our appointment.

"You asked me to come back to discuss the yard work," I offered.

She stood silently, looking at me for what seemed like an eternity, and then she finally said, "Would you like to come upstairs and discuss this with Mother?" She spoke with a great eloquence and with an oddly familiar phrasing. Where had I heard that type of dialect before? It was very smooth—almost sing-song-like—yet with a slight edge. I nodded my head and said, "Yes," excited— and scared—to be asked inside her home. She stepped back and allowed me to enter.

As I stepped across the threshold, I was immediately hit by it: the *smell*. It was overpowering. It was a mix of dirt and mold, but mostly cats, or more accurately— ammonia. It almost knocked me over! As I steadied myself, my eyes soon began to sting from the assault on my senses, but I did my best to keep focused straight ahead as the woman led me up the staircase. I was too wound up to let anything ruin this adventure; I couldn't believe that I had gotten this far! As I made my way to the staircase, I suddenly felt cobwebs laying all over my face, my eyes, and my hair. I tried to avoid being seen wiping them away for fear that I might insult her and be asked to leave. I wasn't about to let *anything* stop me now. Something inexplicable was pushing me forward; I had to find out what mysteries this house held.

The handrail on the staircase was covered in dust; layers upon layers of thick, clumpy, stuff that carpeted everything in sight. It clung to the banister, the rails, and the side tables we passed. Even the stairs beneath me were covered in dust, except for that small well-worn pathway that we were now following.

Suddenly, a voice called out, strong and clear, from the second floor. "Edie!" I was startled. *That must be Mother*, I thought as we reached the landing. For an older person, she had projection!

The woman leading me upstairs called back, "The Marble Faun wants to speak with you, Mother." (Ah, so the woman's name was Edie.) She then led me down a long, dark hall toward a lighted doorway at the end. I followed closely behind, not nervous exactly but excited by this adventure. Once we reached the lighted room, there seated in a reclining chaise lounge was Mother. She was wearing a large brimmed hat, the kind that was designed to be worn at the beach. It was definitely very stylish— twenty or thirty years before! She appeared to be around seventy, with loose, pale skin sagging around her upper arms and uncovered legs. And yet she seemed almost... regal? It was the way she sat. No, reclined. There was an elegance about it. She slowly lifted her head up and her bright blue eyes met mine with a penetrating gaze. She stared at me for a few moments and then said, "You need to eat a boiled potato, chicken breast, and a green salad to keep that beautiful face."

The oddness of this remark surprised me, so I just

THE MARBLE FAUN OF GREY GARDENS

stood there not knowing what to say. I looked to Edie to see her reaction, but she was gone. I turned back to Mother who smiled. "Come and sit down, young man," she said and gestured to a small folding chair in the corner. As I approached it, the cats that were scampering around the floor near her feet and along the baseboards of the room began moaning and crying, clearly agitated by my presence. There must have been twenty of them scurrying about, leaping on a chest of draws and hiding under the bed frame that had no mattress. I love animals, but this felt overwhelming. How did they care for so many cats?

As I sat down, I took the opportunity to survey the room for the first time. Overhead there were large holes in the ceiling, with wooden beams exposed. I could see the roof of the house through the attic, and then I saw what looked to me to be shiny, black pointed noses. It took me a second before I realized they *were* noses – they were raccoons and their black eyes were peering down at us from the floor above. I was frightened for a second, but tried to remain calm, as if this were nothing out of the ordinary. I guess Mother was giving me a chance to absorb it all, because for a few moments we didn't say a word.

"Where do you live young man?" she finally asked.

Startled, I said, "Oh, I work down Lily Pond Lane, at the Geddes estate. I'm an assistant gardener there." I moved in closer to where she was seated so that we could talk more easily.

She reached over to pick up a small radio that was at

her side and began turning the dial, although there was nothing but static. We sat silently for a bit, but even though we were strangers, it didn't feel odd. I felt quite relaxed. There was something comforting about her presence, an ease and naturalness to just sitting together. It seemed as if we had known each other for a long time, as if she were a member of my family.

I decided now was the time to broach the topic of why I was there in the first place. "I've some skills with gardening and I'd like to be of help to you."

She looked at me and smiled. "What is your name, young man?"

I was embarrassed. In the excitement of the situation, I had forgotten to introduce myself.

"Gerard. Torre ... um, Jerry."

"I'm Mrs. Edith Bouvier Beale," she said, "and my daughter is also named Edith. To keep us straight, we call her Edie."

As if on cue, Edie entered the room and I stood up.

"My name is Jerry Torre," I said to Edie. "I work for Mr. Gerald Geddes down Lily Pond Lane."

"Yes," Mrs. Beale said, "we are familiar with Mr. Geddes."

There was an awkward silence as the two women looked at each other. It felt as if there was a story behind these looks, but none was offered. Then Edie let out a quick and girlish giggle, turned, and was out the door again.

"Jerry," Mrs. Beale began, "you have the face of a young girl. In fact, you resemble my own mother, Maude."

It felt a bit odd to hear that I resembled a girl, more so someone's mother. Yet in a strange way it helped me feel even a bit more comfortable. "Yes. The matriarch of the Bouvier family. Maybe you were sent to me by my dear mother?" she said, a twinkle in her eye. "Then there was my father, the Major," she continued. "He would enter the driveway, spinning tires on his automobile, and sending gravel everywhere. He was no driver!"

Suddenly Edie returned. "His daily routine of bathing was awful," Edie offered. "He would set out a full bathtub with ice and add cold water. Then after his morning jog, he would lower himself into the bath tub and belt out this awful cry. My grandmother would command respect at each lunch, breakfast, and dinner. We Bouviers are rather loud when we all gather. Only when Grandmother Maude was present would everyone calm down."

"Edie," Mrs. Beale interrupted, "have you fed the kitties yet? They need to eat, you know."

Edie shook her head and mumbled something I couldn't make out.

"Go and feed the cats while I talk with Mr. Gerard Torre on my own, please."

Edie turned and exited the room again, and as she walked down the hallway, she called out to the cats that it was time to eat.

We sat there for a long while in silence, alone in the room that the Beales referred to as the "Sunroom" because of the second-floor porch that was just outside the door. (Later, it became known as "The Pink Room," where Mrs.

Beale and Edie had one of their most heated disagreements in the film *Grey Gardens*.) After a few minutes, I stood up and approached the door leading to the porch.

"That is our new porch. It was built by the men who tore down the original porch." Mrs. Beale said as I peered outside through the screen door.

I could see that the porch was covered partially in vines; the same vines that covered the front of the mansion and that were ever encroaching on the mansion, threatening to literally rip it apart. It was also home to more cats, or "kitties," as Mrs. Beale referred to them. One sat on top of the farthest railing, another nearby, one group of about four, and an orange tabby looking up at me. The orange tabby looked very much like one of the "kitties" I'd seen as I was walking up the stairway with Edie earlier. At that time, I had seen more of these cats perched along the banister; "tomcats" who were not especially easy to approach (if one had the foolish inclination to try). They roosted everywhere on each landing of the staircase, and where you couldn't see them, you could hear them—and smell them.

"Let's go onto the porch," Mrs. Beale said. "It's ridiculous to stay inside. It's an absolutely beautiful day."

As she began to stand up, I instinctively reached out and took her hand. She looked up at me with affection. "Thank you, dear," she said and we ventured out onto the porch where I helped her into a rattan rocking chair.

For the first time, I looked out onto the expanse of property and was stunned by what I saw. There were no grounds visible—just trees stretching out to the horizon. For a moment, I wondered just what I had gotten myself into. Could I do this all by myself? I turned back to Mrs. Beale and we began to discuss what exactly I could do to help them as a gardener. I said that I would like to start by clearing a path in the front lawn of the property so that it was easier to reach the house from the driveway. We decided that I would return the following morning and begin work. She asked me what she could offer me as a payment for helping. I immediately shook my head. "No, no money," I told her. I didn't need any money and I wasn't doing this for money. I just wanted to help out, and I would enjoy it. She smiled at me once more.

When I stood, Mrs. Beale reached out and gently clasped my hand. I looked into her eyes and said, "I will see you tomorrow morning."

"Yes, little Jerry," she said with a sly smile. "May I call you that?"

"Of course, Mrs. Beale. Can I help you back into the house?"

"No, dear," she said, still smiling. "I'm like a big kitty. I love to feel the sun on my face too. You go ahead and Edie will show you out."

Edie was nowhere to be found as I approached the stairway, which was fine, as I could certainly let myself out. Besides, I had gotten the distinct impression that she was not in the most amiable of moods. (I would find during my days at Grey Gardens that this was often the case; Edie's moods were varied and unpredictable, and they could turn on a dime.)

As I made my way down the staircase, I looked below into the first-floor rooms that I had not seen on my way up the stairs. To my right, as I descended the staircase, was the dining room. Its ceiling had collapsed, and it lay across the expanse of the room. Inside the dining room, there were two large piles of garbage as tall as six feet or more. They were dozens of cans of some sort, piled high in the room, and looked as if they would topple over at any moment. The room was dark despite the bright summer sunlight. The thick patch of vines that covered the windows almost completely shut out the light. The shadows they cast into the room gave it a spooky and surreal atmosphere.

When I reached the bottom of the steps, I turned around and there, standing directly behind me, was Edie. I tried my best not to appear startled. She looked at me intently. Her eyes, like her mother's, were a beautiful deep blue; but unlike her mother's, they were sharp and piercing. When she looked at you, it felt as if she was looking inside you, inspecting your very soul. I smiled at her and said, "Oh, I didn't see you there. I think I should be going. I told your mother I would be back tomorrow."

Edie smiled and walked past me toward the door. She reached for the doorknob, unlocked the brass lock, and without a word, opened the door for me to exit. I thanked her for allowing me the opportunity to come and visit as I stepped onto the front porch. The warm, clean air was so refreshing that I took a deep breath.

"We are familiar with your employer," Edie said. "He has been our neighbor for many years." I detected a slight tinge of disapproval in her voice; not toward me but toward Mr. Geddes. I was not sure exactly how to respond. She stood in the doorway with her arms crossed. "How is it you came to work for him in East Hampton?"

I gave her the briefest rundown: growing up in Brooklyn, coming out to work on my uncle's house from the time I was a child, and the great love for nature that inspired me. "I love the open air here," I said, "the ocean … the beautiful land out here. It's a lot different from Brooklyn. I even like the potato farms."

"Ha," Edie chuckled. It made me happy that I'd made her laugh, and I thought to myself, "You better leave now while you've got her laughing." I said goodbye and made my way back to my bicycle, quickly jumped on it, and rode away from the mansion. My mind was spinning from what I'd just experienced—how would I ever explain it to anyone? Would they even believe me if I did? Even though I had just experienced it, I still couldn't completely believe it all myself.

When I reached the Geddes estate, I noticed Mr. Geddes' large black car sitting in the driveway, alerting me that he was home. I quickly steered my bicycle around to the back of the mansion where I could enter through the kitchen undetected, in keeping with Mr. Geddes' command never to be seen. Charlotte was standing at the entrance to the kitchen wearing her white wrap-around apron, her standard uniform. We all had uniforms we were to wear while performing our duties. Mine consisted of coveralls, yet I rarely wore them when I worked around the yard. I reasoned that since I was to make sure I was never seen by any of the family, no one would notice me in a T-shirt and shorts that were so much more comfortable in the hot afternoon sun. Charlotte greeted this habit of mine with an amused disapproval.

I couldn't wait to tell her where I had just been. "I visited the secret place!" I said to her as I walked into the kitchen. I had told her of my fascination with the Beale's house that day I had discovered it. Although she warned me against exploring it any further, I had to tell her what had happened. "I just spent the morning with the two women who live in the forgotten mansion."

Charlotte followed behind me. "You mean the Cat Ladies?" she said, her voice raising in disbelief.

"Yes." I said, giggling at the nickname.

The nickname "Cat Ladies" had been given to the Beales by the neighborhood children, who, Edie told me later, would often call out when they saw her, "Mommy, look! It's the Cat Lady!" It was a statement that she would hear often when she was out on the front porch, or on one of her infrequent trips into the village. Soon, I discovered the nickname was one that was well known throughout the community of East Hampton. I had seen the dozens of cats inside the mansion at my visit, but, according to Charlotte, at night the cats converged on the street outside the house, making it nearly impossible for a car to drive down the street—there were that many! And despite the fact that the Beales were well known in East Hampton, nobody seemed to know them personally, or be brave enough to approach the house and go inside. So, my adventure was riveting to Charlotte and she wanted details.

I explained to her how it all came about and she seemed stunned by my adolescent nerve and naivety in actually going up to the mansion.

"After I knocked on the door, the younger of the two women—the daughter, Edie—came down the main staircase and opened the door and we talked," I said.

"Well," Charlotte replied with a huff, "you may be interested to know that Mr. Geddes once saw that woman—Edie—socially."

I was astounded. "You mean they dated?" I was a bit taken aback. My employer and the woman I just met seemed millions of miles apart; at the same time, it didn't seem that farfetched. Mr. Geddes, with his odd behaviors and mood swings, could be considered an eccentric, and I saw the traces of a once beautiful woman beneath Edie's unusual appearance.

Charlotte went on to tell me more about the Beales and their history with the Village of East Hampton. To say they were not liked was to put it mildly. According to Charlotte, the village had been attempting to get the Beales evicted for years, since their home was considered an eyesore and an embarrassment to the community. But the Beale's history in East Hampton was deep-rooted, and the community felt they could go only so far in attempting to remove them. Over the years, the residents had developed a tolerance for their eccentric neighbors—some compassionate souls had even taken to leaving a turkey on the front porch at Thanksgiving and Christmas—but make no mistake, the vast majority of the people of East Hampton would have much preferred the Beales vacate their premises to make way for more "acceptable" tenants.

"So," she concluded, "I think it may be best if you made sure Mr. Geddes doesn't find out where you were today."

I nodded in agreement. To have him find out about my visit with the Beales—not to mention my offer to help them on their property—could have aggravated my mercurial employer just enough to fire me. I wouldn't say a thing, I assured Charlotte, and she promised that the details of my new adventure would be our little secret.

CHAPTER THREE: TENDING THE GARDEN

The morning after my first visit with the Beales, I quickly went through my chores on the Geddes estate. It was an easy task since the grounds had been well-patterned and laid out long before I arrived, and my work of mowing the lawn and raking the cuttings took but an hour or two every other day. The gardens that dotted the property were easily maintained, too; fence-roses, some wisteria bushes with purple flowers, and the intermittent tulip bed were all that I really had to concern myself with sustaining. I was done by late morning and was free to slip out to visit Grey Gardens.

Although, I didn't yet know that "Grey Gardens" was the name of my mysterious new surroundings; I found that out after my first months with the Beales, when I heard Edie call it that. When I asked her about it, she said the name was given to the house by a local gardener who noticed that the delphiniums that were planted alongside of other annuals just did not adapt to the sea-environment. These flowers would eventually wilt under the stress of the salt air before they reached full growth, leaving the flowers colorless and grey—thus the name "Grey Gardens." Had the gardener been able to see into the future, to the great state of deterioration that would befall the house, he would have been amazed by his prescience.

Clearly, this was once a grand mansion; the imposing façade, the magnificent skeleton of the rose garden on the mansion's south lawn, the sheer sweep of acreage butting up against Long Island Sound, all impressed me. If it were possible to see beyond the dirt, cobwebs, and decay, the cats and raccoons, past the towers of garbage and debris—you could still find evidence of its splendor. I found this to be true of Mrs. Beale and Edie as well. Despite the situation they found themselves in, and the sometimes outlandish behavior they sometimes exhibited, there was in each of them the lingering aura of a once elegant existence. It was this remarkable quality that I found incredibly appealing. Some called the Beales crazy, but I found their eccentricities touching and more than a little endearing. Here, in this seemingly most unlikely of places, I found peace. I was home.

Of course, the overwhelming assault on my physical senses took some getting used to. Years and years of cats making Grey Gardens their own luxurious litterbox had certainly taken their toll and I had to make sure that when I worked indoors it was in a well-ventilated area. Because I worked primarily as a groundskeeper, though, more of my time was spent outside battling the overgrown vegetation more than inside battling the overpowering smells. I loved the jungle-like atmosphere that had developed on the grounds of the house; at times, I played Tarzan by grabbing onto a thick branch of wisteria and swinging from one overgrown bush to the next. I made much of my work a game, and I was young enough to have an endless supply of energy to tackle each new and overwhelming task. Moreover, after the madness of my violent childhood, I reveled in the calm of my surroundings and felt safe amongst the overgrown wisteria and cans of cat food piled higher than I, or anyone else, could reach on foot.

But mostly, of course, there was Mrs. Beale and Edie's fascinating joy of living that made life at Grey Gardens so enthralling for this inhibited kid from Brooklyn. For someone so curious about life and all it had to offer, to be admitted to this strange and exotic new world was an embarrassment of riches to me, believe it or not. I felt every moment spent with these two remarkable women was one to be experienced fully and cherished.

My first few days working at the Beales' mansion consisted primarily of getting my head around just what it was I had signed up for. To say that my work was "cut out for me" was an understatement of monumental proportion.

But what of my new friends whose lives I was about to enter? Youth—and ignorance—can be a blessing, and I admit that I knew very little about the Beales; just their names and the fact that they needed me. At the time, that was all I needed to know. But who were they and how did they end up the way they did?

Edith Ewing Bouvier was born on October 5, 1895 to John Vernou Bouvier Jr., and Maude Sergeant Bouvier. Mrs. Beale was preceded by two elder brothers, John Vernou III (nicknamed "Black Jack" in later years and father to Jacqueline Kennedy and Lee Radziwill) and William "Bud" Bouvier, then followed by two sisters, Maude and Michelle. From a young age, Mrs. Beale displayed a singular individualistic temperament that may best be described as "artistic." She also exhibited an exceptional musicality, and her mother, sensing this special talent, indulged her to the extent that she soon developed an outsized and flamboyant demeanor more befitting an operatic soprano than a demur debutante from one of America's premiere families. While her mother may have indulged her, Mrs. Beale's father, acutely aware of his family's social standing, found his daughter's behaviors embarrassing and unacceptable. His fears were lessened somewhat by Edith's 1916 engagement to a high-powered corporate attorney—and his future law partner—Phelean Beale, son of a respected southern family and twenty years Edith's senior. Their marriage on January 17, 1917 was a highlight of the New York social season; an elaborate affair held at St Patrick's Cathedral with over 2,000 invited guests.

Later that same year, Mrs. Beale gave birth to a girl, Edith Bouvier Beale, on November 7, 1917, followed by two boys: Phelean Jr., in 1920, and two years later, Bouvier

Beale, also known as "Buddy," followed. From what Mrs. Beale told me, she loved being a mother, but she felt more and more unfulfilled in her life as "Mrs. Phelan Beale," and the old artistic impulses she had been suppressing during her marriage began stirring within her.

With a nurse and her mother to care for the children, Mrs. Beale began to focus attentions on her desire to perform, something that her husband could not understand or appreciate any more than her father did. In response to his disapproval, she became increasingly avant-garde in dress and philosophy, shocking many by surrounding herself with the various artists, writers, and theatrical personalities with whom she felt a kindred spirit. She invited this contingent of bohemians—many of whom were openly and flamboyantly gay, she said—to the frequent teas and salons she threw at her New York apartment. In 1923, Phelan Sr., purchased a beautiful home in East Hampton as a gift for his wife. It was designed as a summer retreat for the family, but it soon became Mrs. Beale's private theatre. In time, every social event held there became an excuse for a mini-concert. This, as well as her growing collection of odd and "unacceptable" associates, grew increasingly irritating to the prestige-conscious Phelean, and, as a result, he began absenting himself from Grey Gardens—and from his marriage.

All the while, "Little Edie," as the Beale's daughter was nicknamed, was blossoming into a stunning young woman: tall, blonde, with large, bright blue eyes and—as Edie recalled a society journalist once writing—"the longest black eyelashes you've ever seen." When she was a teenager, society columns nicknamed her "Body Beautiful Beale," and she modeled at charity fashion shows in both New York City and East Hampton. When we were alone, and out of Edie's earshot, Mrs. Beale would tell me how popular Edie was in these years; how at all the fashionable dances and events she was the "belle of the ball"—in high demand as a companion and dancing partner.

In addition to her physical beauty, Edie had a sharp and sensitive mind. Like her mother, she possessed a strong yearning for expression in the creative arts, and she frequently professed a desire for a career as an actress, a poet, or a dancer. As her mother had done with her, Mrs. Beale encouraged her daughter's artistic aspirations to the point of overindulgence to some disapproving onlookers, most notably her husband. Dressed in velvet coats and lace-trimmed socks, Edie was her mother's constant companion to society lunches and charity events, and Mrs. Beale frequently removed her from classes at the Spence School to accompany her to the theater, movies, and, on more than one occasion, shopping trips to Paris. Mr. Beale was aghast since such behavior indicated to him that his daughter would follow in her mother's eccentric, and unacceptable, footsteps. He expected nothing less from his daughter than her becoming a junior partner in his law firm or—at the very least—becoming a wife to one. To assure this end, he curbed her literary aspirations by criticizing her grammar and diction. In order to squash her dreams of being a great dancer, he ordered that she wear clunky, unattractive orthopedic shoes. When a photographer's advertisement for which Edie had posed found its way to the front window of a Madison Avenue store, Mr. Beale shattered the display glass and removed it. His attempts to manage his young daughter's life bordered on dictatorial cruelty and struck a terror in Edie from which she never fully recovered.

As for Mrs. Beale, her husband could no longer tolerate what he perceived as a complete lack of respect for him and their social position. By 1934, the differences in their outlooks on life were total and irreconcilable, and the couple separated; he, residing in the family's Manhattan apartment and she, ensconced securely away from his disapproving eyes at Grey Gardens. Though still legally married, Mrs. Beale received only child support from her husband, so a financial burden fell upon Mrs. Beale's father for additional support for the household. This added more tension to an already strained relationship between father and daughter, but Mrs. Beale told me that she finally felt free to live her life as she wished. Once and for all, she rejected the revered conventions of her social class and began living according to her own private desires. She rejected her family's Catholicism, refused to have her name included in the social register, chose with whom she wished to associate regardless of their standing in society, and challenged her family's beliefs, habits, and codes of conduct frequently and vociferously. By the time of her divorce from Mr. Beale in 1946, she had alienated herself from her family to such an extent that she withdrew completely and began living in virtual reclusion at Grey Gardens. She said that she preferred it that way.

Because of her great beauty and pedigree, Edie was a virtual magnet for many of the sons of affluence of the day, including Joseph Kennedy, Jr. Elliot Roosevelt and Howard Hughes. (About the latter, Mrs. Beale once told me that Edie stopped seeing the famous aviator because she found his well-known eccentricities too odd!) For reasons that she never fully explained to me, Edie rejected all prospects of marriage, and then World War II intervened and effectively ended her days as the "golden child." By the end of the war, twenty-seven-year-old Edie found herself alone with her mother, many of her previous suitors either married or casualties of the war.

With her father and his crushing disapproval at a safe distance (he remarried quickly after his divorce from Mrs. Beale), Edie set her sights on the theatrical career she had always longed for and she moved to New York City, where she took up residence at the Barbizon, a well-known woman's hotel. The difficulties of an aspiring performer's life, as well as the continual demand from her mother to return home, slowly wore down her already shaky self-confidence. After a few years on her own, she gave in to her mother's pleas. She checked out of the Barbizon on July 29, 1952, left New York City, and returned to Grey Gardens.

Of course, I didn't find out this "backstory" until many months later, in bits and pieces that I had to string together. The past was subjective and ever changing at Grey

Gardens, and the truth of what happened to the Beales to bring them to their present state seemed at times to be as intricate and multi-layered as the cobwebs that surrounded us. At first, I was curious and eager to solve the mystery of their past; in time, however, I realized that the pursuit of answers was not only futile but inconsequential. How they came to destitution didn't really matter, especially if they didn't wish to discuss it. Besides, at no point did I see either of them show any disgust or dismay for their extreme living conditions. For the Beales, all the trash and dirt and dust was normal. Whatever existed for them in the former life was gone and so they moved on as best as they could and in the only way they knew how. Revisiting the past didn't change the present—and the present was fascinating enough, believe me.

In many ways, the mansion itself was as much a "character" as the Beales. Although many people are familiar with the house from the documentary movie, you really had to be there in person to fully appreciate it. I always thought that Grey Gardens was a metaphor for the Beale's themselves, and just as fascinating. Upon entering through the front entry, you stood in the vestibule (the area in which Edie does her "VMI March" in *Grey Gardens*). The vestibule, like everywhere else, was draped with cobwebs. There was an enormous mirror hanging on the wall that was covered with so much dust that it ceased to be reflective. Because of the large holes in the roof and ceilings throughout the house, the walls had all been saturated with rain water and had begun to disintegrate. Directly across from the main entrance, underneath the staircase, was a small alcove draped in a gold brocaded cloth. Behind the gold drape, I discovered a doorway that led out to the garden behind the house; this was once the gardener's entrance. Next to the doorway was a small washroom that had a three-pronged pewter lamp hanging over a small sink that would have been used by the grounds people to wash.

To the right of the main entrance was the library, now crammed with piles of empty cat food cans and other refuse that reached almost to the ceiling. Bookshelves lined the walls of the room—many of the books had been signed by John Vernor Bouvier (I had not yet learned of Mrs. Beale's famous lineage, so this name meant nothing to me at first). Faded floral draperies hung next to the windows that looked out onto the front porch, each covered by a simple pull-down shade. There was a rain-soaked table covered with white mold, its legs carved in a pineapple pattern. Years of rain and snow blowing through the warped and broken windows had dry-rotted practically all the floorboards as well as any furniture in the room. Near the entrance to the library there was a large grand piano—still, remarkably, in working order—that would occasionally draw the attention of Mrs. Beale should I happen to absent-mindedly strike one of its keys. As the notes echoed through the house, Mrs. Beale would find her way out of the upstairs bedroom and insist that I continue to play (even though I hadn't a clue as to know how). Then, seated aside the banister, she would begin to perform songs from long ago. I came to understand that this piano was "Gould's piano," referring to George Gould Strong, a man who had been Mrs. Beale's accompanist during the glory days of Grey Gardens, when she gave afternoon concerts in the solarium. It was always intimated that his attentions toward her were a major cause in the rift between Mrs. Beale and her husband, Phelan, although she and I never discussed it. It didn't occur to me to ask her about such personal matters in her life as that was not the nature of our relationship. I was raised to respect my elders, and to ask such questions would have been rude and disrespectful. Besides which, from the beginning my feelings for her were of love and concern; I wouldn't have wanted to alienate her and give her cause to regret having allowed me into her life.

There was so much work to be done at Grey Gardens that often I didn't leave until well past midnight, only to have to return the next day to finish up what I had started. After a few weeks of this late-night shuttling back and forth, I asked Mrs. Beale if it would be alright if I just stayed overnight at the mansion, as my duties at Geddes in the morning were not pressing. She agreed, and I soon made the library my "home base."

The focal point of the library was a large fireplace that was situated on the wall opposite the entrance to the room. One particularly cold night during my first winter at the house, I entertained the notion of cleaning out the hearth and setting a fire—but suddenly I had a vision of the entire mansion in flames, and I quickly dismissed such thoughts. (In fact, I made it a point to never even strike a match inside the mansion; the potential for setting the entire place afire was so great.) As additional shelter, I draped a painter's tarp across Gould's piano and nailed an end to the bookshelves, creating a makeshift tent with an opening just narrow enough for me to place an army cot.

Standing next to the fireplace was a large triangular object that I can only describe as looking like a six-foot tall cone of cotton candy. A few weeks after I began visiting the mansion, I worked up the courage to gingerly approach the object, not wanting to disturb the dust or any creatures that may be calling it home. I took a deep breath (not too deep!) and reached inside the cobwebs. Suddenly, I heard glass shattering as something fell to the wooden floor. I recoiled and stepped back. Looking down, I saw at my feet the remains of a glass ornament; this cotton candy object was a fully decorated Christmas tree! Who knows how many Christmases had passed since it had been put up and trimmed, but the layers of dust and cobwebs had covered the branches to the point that it was unrecognizable.

Just to the left of the hearth was the solarium. Many of the panes of glass were broken, allowing the elements free reign inside. There was a bed frame, completely rusted, sitting in the middle of the room. Dangling from the rafters above were remains of clay pots that I imagined once overflowed with geraniums, philodendrons, or bougainvillea. Instead, dry brown vines were interwoven up and around the pots, in and out, like a crazy woven basket. There was a door at the far end of the solarium that led outside to what was, at one time, a small garden. After years of unrestrained growth, however, it was now an overgrown jungle of English Ivy, Virginia creeper (also known a Trumpet Vine), Poison Ivy, grapevines, and several other wild types of vegetation. Moreover, this section of the mansion had a southern exposure, and with the additional sunlight, the overgrowth of wisteria and bittersweet ran riot. I attempted to open the door to go into the garden, but it wouldn't budge. The bittersweet vine had swollen to the width of a small tree trunk, and its branches twisted and wrapped around the outside walls of the house. If one was of an inquisitive nature, as I clearly was, he or she could follow the vine and wisteria from their point of origin at the foot of the solarium, around and up, twisting higher and higher up the side of the house and snaking under the eaves of the top floor and inside the house, meandering through rotted timbers until it traversed the entire span of the attic. Once there, it literally lifted the roof off the house.

This disastrous state of affairs was repeated from room to room throughout the mansion; from the library where the rain-soaked ceiling had collapsed, creating an unintended two-story skylight up through the master bedroom and into the attic, to the "Old Dining Room," as Mrs. Beale called it, but which I began to refer to as a "disposal room" due to the piles of cascading rubbish. (I feel it is important to point out that Mrs. Beale and Edie did this only out of necessity. There was no public sanitation program in East Hampton, and having long ago run out of funds to pay for private sanitation pick up, they were left with no choice but to dispose of the accumulated rubbish themselves.) This room also had a fireplace with a long mantel on which Edie had collected a collage of items ranging from broken pieces of china, glass figurines, and a picture of late President John F. Kennedy. Also in the room, but concealed behind piles of debris, was a built-in china cabinet, the contents of which included a few Faberge eggs, a set of Wedgewood china, and Mrs. Beale's beloved green goblets. Apparently, these few precious items were all that remained of a once fabulous collection of valuables that had been sold off over the years.

On the side of the dining room, opposite the vestibule, was the small butler's pantry that contained, among many cabinets, a long-abandoned dumbwaiter. It had two elaborately carved swinging doors on it and when opened, revealed not only the wheeled dumbwaiter apparatus, but a pass through to the kitchen. Though the waiter itself was frozen between floors, the shaft was still being used as a method of transport of food—although not by humans; the raccoons, who had long ago been allowed in the house and virtually domesticated by Edie and Mrs. Beale, used it as a food thoroughfare. Buster (Edie's favorite raccoon) and his friends would carry whatever food Edie would leave out for them from the attic and down through the dumbwaiter to the first floor and basement. Their "meals" consisted of anything from loaves of white bread and dry cat food to the Fudge Royal Ice Cream that Mrs. Beale would order from the local Newtown Grocers. I must say that throughout the years I lived there, I never quite got accustomed to the nightly ritual of feeding the raccoons— they were a bit too "comfortable" in their residence. But, as with everything that happened at Grey Gardens, I deferred to Mrs. Beale and her wishes. I did my best to steer clear of the raccoons, who were nocturnal anyway and rarely came out during the day. On those nights when I stayed over, usually in that makeshift tent that I had set up in the library, I would hear them tearing into any food that may have been left lying about the house. On one occasion, I awoke in the middle of the night to find my pant legs being gnawed at by a raccoon in search of chewing gum or food I may have left in my pockets. Needless to say, I learned quickly to empty my pockets at bedtime. I also kept a brass poker from the fireplace next to my tent just in case.

Exiting the butler's pantry, one found a long corridor that ran to the rear of the house with three doors aside its length, the first leading to the kitchen. Just inside the kitchen stood "Perfection," so named by its manufacturer. Perfection was the largest wood-and-coal-burning stove I had ever seen; its sheer weight was such that it had begun to sink through the decaying kitchen floor and into the cellar below. It was clear that the kitchen had not been used for years—perhaps decades—and the north facing exterior kitchen wall buckled from rot and frequently swayed with the winds coming in from the ocean.

People have often asked me if there were any working

bathrooms at the house. The truth was that there were two bathrooms that were still in working order, one on the second floor of the house and a smaller one on the first floor adjacent to the back porch. This smaller bathroom had only a toilet and a sink, and it was mine to use when I stayed at the mansion. The second-story bathroom had the only working bathtub in the house and was used by Edie, who on more than one occasion caused a flood when she neglected to remove her homemade stopper—crumpled newspaper—from the tub, and she would absentmindedly leave the spigot running.

Shuttling between my two "homes"—for that is what I began to consider Grey Gardens—became my daily ritual. The liberation from my past, the abundance of having not one but two amazing places to call home, added a certain magic to my life. By this time, contact with my biological family was sporadic and consisted of no more than an occasional phone call to my mother. Though being away from her was painful, I knew that visiting her involved dealing with my father. That was out of the question. And while my heart ached to know what she was going through with him, she refused to leave her husband. As she told me on the many occasions that I had pleaded with her to leave him, this was her life; I had to live my own.

Each visit to Grey Gardens was so entertaining, even if Mrs. Beale was of limited mobility. She was, I discovered, a virtual invalid. Among the ailments that plagued her were high-blood pressure, cataracts, glaucoma, and perhaps the most serious of all, gout. It was because of this joint-stiffening malady that movement was difficult and painful for her, and she confined herself to a few rooms on the second floor of the mansion: the sunroom, its adjacent porch, and her bedroom—a small room in the center of the upstairs hallway that she and Edie shared. They had moved into this room sometime in the late 1960s when the furnace in the mansion ceased working and a room was needed that was small enough to be warmed by a space heater but also close to the bathroom. Edie referred to this room as the "Center Bedroom" because of its location in the house, but it was also an appropriate name as it was the epicenter of the household. It was where, in other words, all the action took place.

Here, every great drama was played out, every malicious conspiracy suspected was investigated, and every minutia of day to day life was dissected and analyzed. It was also where Mrs. Beale held court, where her counsel was sought, and where all important decisions were made. To me, this was my favorite room because it was where Mrs. Beale basically lived, and it is where I have my most beloved memories of our time together. We sang, told stories, and shared meals in that room. Mostly we just spent time together, and I cherished Mrs. Beale's company. With each visit, the trust between us grew. I was so honored that these two reclusive people allowed me into their private world. I know that for some people the extreme and bizarre world of Grey Gardens would have been too much to take, but for me, it was very exciting.

All my life I longed to be a part of a loving family where the threat of violence wasn't lurking behind every corner. I found that at Grey Gardens. From the moment Edie first opened the door, I was a welcomed into this special "family," which meant more than I can convey.

Which is not to say that my days there were not without challenges. Though it was Edie who initially welcomed me into the mansion, I believe that my growing closeness with her mother threatened her. And she often let her feelings be known in odd and frustrating ways.

Many times, that first summer, I would arrive at the house and Edie would refuse to let me in, no matter how many entreaties I made. When this happened, I would call out to Mrs. Beale from beneath her window, and usually she would order Edie to let me in—but a few times my calls went unanswered. In these instances, I would eventually give up and go back to Geddes, only to return the next day to be greeted by Edie as if nothing had happened. There were other days when I would overhear Edie brewing up some untruth about me, as if to discourage Mrs. Beale's growing friendship with me. However, the bond that was growing between Mrs. Beale and myself was becoming so strong that Edie's accusations against me never went very far with her mother. Mrs. Beale and I loved each other like a mother and son, and it was as simple as that. I can only guess that it was this growing affection between myself and her mother that may have caused Edie to act out against me in this way; I cannot think of any other reason for some of her erratic behaviors toward me. But then again, I witnessed her behaving this same way with other people as well, and without these motivations to justify her actions. I came to realize and accept that this was just Edie being Edie, and I didn't let it bother me or affect my growing love for Mrs. Beale.

Looking back, I often wonder if I was filling a void left in Mrs. Beale's life by the absence of her sons. I knew very little about them at this point, except the fact that they were not around. Edie would often mention one of them in passing—but it was always in terms of the past, such as "When my brothers and I were children." Mrs. Beale would only refer to them in the most glowing of terms, and it was usually to condemn Edie's behavior. "My sons would never treat me in such a callous manner," she said one morning after a particularly chilly night during which she accused Edie of leaving her without any blankets on the bed. "Your sons wouldn't care at all!" Edie bellowed back from the downstairs hallway. I chuckled to myself, as I knew that Mrs. Beale in fact had more than enough blankets lying at the foot of her bed; I made sure of it before I'd left that night. She was just in a mood to harass Edie. "Oh, Jerry," she said, looking over at me, "I'm treated very badly. I'm so glad you're here to look after me." Whether or not it was true, it certainly made me feel as if I were a loving son.

In fact, I took the bold step that first year of asking Mrs. Beale—in front of Edie—if I could call her "Mother." This may seem like a pretty forward thing for me to do, but my feelings for Mrs. Beale were so strong that I simply could not imagine my life without her, nor did I want to. Calling her Mother seemed natural and right; in every way, she became my surrogate mother. Though I was on my own, I was still only a teenager and deep inside I yearned for the love and acceptance of a mother, something that I never really received from my own. I don't blame my mother; she was much too busy dealing with my father's abuse. But a boy needs a mother's love, and thankfully Mrs. Beale provided that at precisely the very moment in which I needed it most. Mrs. Beale's reaction to my proposal was one of immediate joy and acceptance, at which point I approached her and kissed her very gently on the right cheek. Later, it occurred to me that it may have been the first demonstration of affection that Mrs. Beale had known in some years. Seeing this tender exchange, Edie, rather than being upset, appeared surprisingly jubilant— jumping up and down and clapping her hands in delight at the exchange of affection. She was, if anything, unpredictable.

After a time, I came to expect the unpredictability of Edie's nature and became accustomed to it. I realized that her bizarrely competitive edge was in her mind alone, and that Mrs. Beale paid little or no attention to Edie's flights of fancy. Any seeds of mistrust about me that she attempted to plant in Mrs. Beale's mind never went anywhere. After witnessing Mrs. Beale's dismissive reaction to Edie's tall tales, I adopted the same attitude. Whenever I felt myself pulled in by one of Edie's dramatic accusations—as when she accused me of stealing from the china cabinet—all I would have to do is look at Mrs. Beale and the faith that I saw displayed in her eyes was all I needed to let the incident go.

Besides, any incidents of theft that I might commit would be for the Beale's benefit, not to their detriment. I admit that there were occasions when, facing dwindling supplies of food at the house, I would make the trip into the village to do some creative "shopping." I would go to the East Hampton IGA supermarket wearing loose dungarees with a thick belt tied around my waist, and then proceed to stuff as many groceries into my pants as possible before making the quick trip back to the mansion. Thankfully, I was never caught, and we would have food in the house for a few more days. Edie never blinked an eye at these occurrences—in fact, she seemed grateful for my resourcefulness. Then, a day later, she would lock me out of the house or accuse me of stealing a book or a knickknack that she had misplaced and the drama would happen all over again. These sudden mood swings were baffling, but I didn't let it bother me too much. I knew a bit about dealing with erratic behavior from the years with my father, and I also knew the best way to deal with it was to remain composed and try to act unaffected. Nevertheless, I confess that I grew very fond of Edie over that first summer and autumn at the mansion. I believe, too, that despite what she may have said about me in her darker moments, that she loved me and appreciated my help at the house.

People have asked if Edie was mentally ill, but I can't

make that statement. To me—and remember, I was quite young at the time—Edie was simply herself. Her odd behaviors were more entertaining than anything else, and I didn't spend much time trying to understand the pathology behind them. But during that first, long winter at Grey Gardens, Mrs. Beale and I had extensive conversations, many about Edie, and that helped me understand a bit more why she was the way she was.

She told me of the difficult time she had when Edie was a young woman and Mrs. Beale was raising her alone. Edie wanted desperately to go back to New York City to pursue her career as an actress, but Mr. Beale did not approve and refused to support Edie in her acting dreams, just as he'd sought to suppress Mrs. Beale as a young woman. Mrs. Beale very much wanted Edie to go after her dreams, but her small allowance left her with barely enough money to support herself in East Hampton, let alone help finance Edie's future. Mrs. Beale said that Edie was in a fury, and made life miserable at Grey Gardens. Finally, she said that she couldn't take it anymore, and told Edie to leave the mansion and go pursue her dreams if she wanted it so badly.

Edie did just that, and though Mrs. Beale did what she could in way of helping out, it became apparent after a year or so on her own in New York that Edie was not doing well. She was ill, Mrs. Beale remarked, and very thin. Not only that, but—and this she told me in a voice just above a whisper—Edie had gotten involved with a married man. She had no choice but to return to East Hampton and her mother's care, where she remained, resentfully.

Over the years, I have come to appreciate what it must have been like for Edie, after all those years alone with her mother, to suddenly have me, a third person, around. It had been nearly twenty years since anyone had even entered Grey Gardens, let alone a young and energetic young man, and the effect must have been both stimulating and frustrating for her. Edie had learned long ago to entertain herself with her imagination, because for the past two decades she had no other company other than her mother. She lived in a private world of illusion for so long that it became her reality, so anything that threatened that fantasy life must have been jarring. To suddenly be confronted with this sixteen-year-old boy trespassing on her world, as well as the closeness of her relationship with her mother, must have been a real threat to her.

I also know, however, that for as many times as she felt challenged by my presence, there were instances when she welcomed it too. There would be days when Edie would disappear for hours at a time, and I knew instinctively that she was seeking refuge somewhere in the house, grateful for a few moments to herself. Often, I would spy her sitting in a rotten red leather chair that was positioned near the gardener's entrance at the rear of the house, quietly engrossed in her thoughts. Edie referred to this chair as "the unseen chair," as it was hidden beneath a canopy of leaves. More than a few times that autumn I remember coming upon Edie sitting in the "unseen chair" appearing to be deep in thought. I was careful not to disturb her, as it was clear that she wished to be left alone. After these episodes, she would usually join Mrs. Beale and me in the upstairs bedroom, her spirit seemed lighthearted and renewed. Those days when she was in a good mood—and there were many—she had a wonderful youthfulness about her. I was shocked when I found out later that her actual age was fifty-five, because often she acted as if she were only a few years older than I. Those occasions when she was happy and playful were grand days indeed. Often, we three would gather in the bedroom and sing and laugh while Mrs. Beale mixed drinks—usually gin gimlets or highballs. I would occasionally have a sip or two, as would Edie. These gatherings were always fun and warm. Perhaps it was the innocence of my youth, but looking back I can say that, for me, there was never a boring day with Mrs. Beale and Edie around. Challenging days, yes—but never boring.

And challenges abounded at Grey Gardens, particularly during my first year. The place was in such a state of disrepair that any headway I made on the grounds was miniscule and barely noticeable. I did manage to clear out the dead and decaying vegetation that overcame the driveway to the house, making it easier for the trucks from Newtown Grocers to make food deliveries. After a great effort, I was also successful in cutting back some of the twisted vines that ran the length of the front porch and threatened to bring it all down. It was yeoman's work to be sure, but it was heaven compared to trying to work inside the house. There were days that summer when the stifling heat slowly baking the house and the ever-lingering scent of cats combined to make such a potent mixture that entering the front door could very nearly knock a person back outside again. To attempt to get some air circulating in the house, I pried open two of the windows in the dining room that weren't warped shut and this helped a little, but Edie forbade me from leaving the front door open out of fear of intruders or vandals. I eventually got to the point where I could tolerate working inside the house for a few hours in the early morning, but it still was not easy.

And the fleas! One day the humid air was so thick that I had decided to roll up my pants as to make them into shorts. Within seconds I was overwhelmed by fleas. The calves of both my legs were covered with them, and I kept sweeping my palm down my calves to wipe them off. They were so numerous, they resembled poppy seeds on a loaf of bread. No matter how much bug spray or flea replant we applied, once an area of flesh was exposed, the fleas would attack. I learned that even on the hottest afternoons I had to keep my legs and arms covered. Edie, on the other hand, was a prime target for attack because of her fondness for short skirts and bathing suits, and she suffered mightily from the constant bites.

One of the chores that I had assumed was feeding the many feral cats that had taken up residence in the mansion. Mrs. Beale and Edie adored their "kitties," and like me, any stray or runaway that showed up at the door was immediately welcomed into the fold. The house cats were usually fed canned cat food or, on occasion, Mrs. Beale's liver pate if the cans got mixed up. The dozens of feral cats that roamed the attic and bowels of the house, however, were another matter. I would contact my friend Bill who lived nearby in Amagansett, and together we would head up to Gardiner's Bay, just north of East Hampton. I had another friend, Darrel, who lived in Lazy Point, and he would let us use his motorboat to go out into the bay and fish for porgies, which are large, fat bottom-dwellers and are plentiful in the waters off Long Island. As soon as Bill and I had made a big haul, we would head to shore and Darrel would escort me back to East Hampton with the bags of fish that we had caught that day.

At the Beale's, I would boil the fish (though sinking into the basement, Perfection still had a functioning stovetop) until the smell overwhelmed the house and you could hear the cats stirring in the attic. Carrying the cooked fish up to one of the upstairs bedrooms, I'd dump the fish in the middle of the floor. I then quickly jumped back as dozens of cats descended like wildfire from the attic through the holes in the bedroom ceiling. It was a feeding frenzy. After the fish were completely devoured, the cats would race back up into the attic and out of sight. It was a thrilling and frightening spectacle to watch; the speed with which they descended from above and the moaning and growling as they devoured their food. It was a little bit like a horror movie. I just made sure that I was as far back as possible for fear of getting caught in their rampage.

There were other perils in addition flea attacks and

feral cats to keep you on your toes. The specter of fire hung over our heads at all times. It wasn't just the trash that littered the mansion that was a threat but the frayed and worn electrical wiring that ran throughout the house. Neither Mrs. Beale nor Edie, however, seemed alarmed. I remember vividly one afternoon that first summer, because if not for some fast action on my part, the name "Grey Gardens" could have taken a very literal meaning. I was down in the library tinkering with Gould's piano when I heard laughter coming from upstairs. I went to see what had Mrs. Beale so amused and I found her cooking on her bed! Since the kitchen had long been non-functioning, the Beales had rigged up a campground-like system of cooking, complete with a portable stove powered by cans of Sterno. This set-up allowed Mrs. Beale to cook in bed. While the scenario frightened me, it was routine and a non-issue for Edie and Mrs. Beale.

That particular afternoon, Mrs. Beale was cooking oatmeal as Edie sat in the corner watching. An old pot with no handle was on the stove-top, with water boiling away furiously. As the boiling water began knocking the pot about, Mrs. Beale fumbled with the lid to keep it closed. Soon the water in the pot began to boil up and over its side, making the flame from the Sterno dance as the water hit it. My mind raced with the thought of fire. As flames began to reach out toward the mattress, I was propelled into action. I quickly grabbed a towel and rushed to extinguish the growing flame. While this was happening, Edie went on and on about how thrilled Mother had become over my tinkering on Gould's piano. She was completely and utterly ignorant of the disaster that had just been averted. For a moment, I stood dumbfounded by Edie. I took a deep breath and said to Mrs. Beale, "Promise me whenever you decide to cook, whether it be oatmeal, a cup of tea, a can of soup, or corn on the cob, promise me you'll call for me so I can be here with you. Please."

She kept that promise ... when she remembered it.

The summer was cooling down and autumn was on its way. I began to witness the migration south of not only the many birds that populate the shores of Georgica Pond but also the many tourists that populate its shores as well. At the Geddes mansion, Charlotte slowly began the process of preparing the house for winter, packing up food and perishable items to ship to New York, covering the tables and chairs with sheets, and making sure all linens were clean and stored away. This was a decades-long ritual and was accomplished by the household staff in a manner of weeks.

At Grey Gardens, things were a different story. The change of the seasons brought its own particular problems, and I grew increasingly concerned about just how the three of us would survive the winter season. Though my job at Geddes was seasonal, Mr. Geddes wanted someone to stay on the grounds to keep an eye on things during the winter months. I was happy to agree to this, even though I knew I would probably be hunkering down more frequently at Grey Gardens than in my warm little bedroom at Geddes. As glorious as the summertime can be out on the shores of Long Island, winter can be brutal, bleak, and long. I couldn't imagine leaving my new family to face it alone.

The Beales had an account at the local hardware store, and I convinced Mrs. Beale that we needed to rent a larger and more powerful portable heater than she currently utilized. With the Sterno episode still burning brightly in my memory, I placed the heater between the twin beds and kept a focused watch as the twists of the electric coils turned pink, then orange, then bright red. Mrs. Beale seemed amused at my vigilance with the heater, but she humored me and made a solemn promise not to tamper with it once I had turned it on. I closed the warped doors of the bedroom closed as tightly as was possible and after fifteen or twenty minutes, the bedroom warmed sufficiently so that I could turn off the heater. The room held the heat for the better part of the night. I decided that I would turn the heater on in the late afternoon, while I was still around and able to keep an eye on it, then before saying goodnight, I would make sure the heater was off and all was safe and warm. Except for those days in which Edie would decide to lock me out of the mansion, I was able to perform this routine daily. We would say our goodnights, I would leave Mrs. Beale and Edie in the security and warmth of the room, and then retreat to cot downstairs. There, I would put on as many layers of clothing as I could, and I would tuck myself into bed covered with as many blankets, newspapers, and towels that I could lay my hands on.

Winter truly made Grey Gardens seem like a desolate

and forlorn place. In the summertime, the lush green overgrowth softened the appearance of the harsh and weather-beaten exterior of the house. The warm summer breezes that whistled through the broken and cracked windows were oddly soothing. In winter, by contrast, there was nothing soft or comforting; every frigid gust of wind was like a slap in the face. There was the occasional snow storm that left a thick blanket of snow over the grounds and gave the place a quiet, serene feel, but usually the grounds remained barren and desolate during these months. The only distraction during these harsh days was the approach of the holidays, and I was excited.

I had spent the previous Thanksgiving by myself, and it was a sad and lonely time. By now, contact with my family was very sporadic. I would occasionally call my mother to check in on her, but I didn't want to give away too much about my living situation away as I was technically still a minor. If they wanted to, my parents could force me to return to them. They knew about my job at Geddes, and I had mentioned the Beales to my mother over the phone. That was a mistake.

A few times during the first year at Grey Gardens, my parents came out to the Beale's house looking for me. When I was there and saw them coming, I ran into the attic to hide. Usually, my mother waited in the car while my father was greeted at the door by Edie. He would proceed to turn all his considerable charm on her in an attempt to obtain information on my whereabouts. To Edie's credit, and my great relief, she always saw through my father's façade and, in turn, played the coquettish enchanter bit for all it was worth, never once giving me away. It takes one to know one, I guess, and they were quite a pair, those two—each trying to out-charm the other. After about twenty minutes, my father would leave and Edie would call out to me that the coast was clear, and I would come down from my hiding place in the attic. For all our differences, I think Edie identified with my conflicted feelings toward my family: my love and concern for my mother, but the fear I felt about ever being in my father's house again. "The family arm is very strong," Edie would sometimes say, and I knew that she was thinking of her own father and mother, the grip of family that still held her in its grasp. Then we would all meet in Mrs. Beale's room for a highball to toast our victory over my father.

The thought of being with my new family over the holidays was exciting to me. At first, the idea of a full-dress, celebratory Thanksgiving feast at one of East Hampton's local restaurants occurred to me. How wonderful it would be to put on our finest gear—whatever that was—and go out into town for a real holiday meal. I was shortly disavowed of this fantasy, however. Oh, there were smiles and some head nodding by Mrs. Beale when I brought up the idea, but as the holiday approached, all my suggestions of restaurants were met with silence. Finally, one week before Thanksgiving, Edie took me aside. "Jerry," she said in a low voice, "you won't ever get Mother to leave the house. Believe me, I've tried for years and years. She won't go. And I couldn't leave her here alone. Not on Thanksgiving."

I must say, I wasn't surprised. As the days wore on, it became clear to me that getting Mrs. Beale out of the house entailed not only physical obstacles but significant mental ones as well. Edie told me that Mrs. Beale hadn't left the grounds in nearly twenty years! I was dumbfounded. That was my entire lifetime, and then some. "Don't worry," Edie then remarked, "someone always leaves a turkey or a chicken for us on the front porch on Thanksgiving. It's the one thing I like about the people of East Hampton. We'll have a nice little celebration."

Sure enough, I arrived at the house the day before Thanksgiving to find a brown paper bag sitting on the front porch. I opened it and inside was a fully-cooked turkey, as well as some mashed potatoes and apple stuffing. I picked up the bag to take it inside to Edie. I had to laugh to myself. Thank goodness the turkey was already cooked. I couldn't imagine attempting to fire up Perfection to accomplish that task.

Though I had accepted the refusal of a Thanksgiving outside the mansion, I had another plan in mind for Christmas. I hadn't experienced a real "family" Christmas for as long as I could remember, as the constant turmoil in my father's house always threatened any meaningful holiday celebration. I was therefore especially looking forward to experiencing Christmas with the Beales. After all, Christmas was about home and family. It was about sitting with your loved ones around a tree, exchanging presents, singing holiday songs. I was sure that Mrs. Beale would enjoy that—particularly singing holiday songs.

As for gifts, I knew that both Edie and Mrs. Beale were fond of a specific bakery in town that made wonderful doughnuts, and I decided I would buy some as a present for our Christmas morning breakfast.

Now, what about a tree? We certainly couldn't use the cobweb-covered Christmas tree in the library. Then it dawned on me—the trees out in the garden! So, one cold afternoon a few days before Christmas, I made my way through the thick brush of the side yard toward the garden wall. Climbing the wall wasn't too difficult; I held a large serrated knife in one hand as I pulled myself up toward the top of the wall with the other, and made my way over and headed toward one particular tree that looked perfect in its size—about four feet tall. Cutting it down was more difficult than I'd thought, due to the sticky sap that flowed from the tree, but I managed the task and dragged the tree back to the front porch where I wiped it clean of sap and dirt. Any regrets that I felt about cutting down this beautiful, living piece of nature were swept aside when I thought of the joy it would bring my friends inside.

I carried the tree into the house and up to Mrs. Beale's room. Both she and Edie were delighted, and Edie immediately began running about to look for decorations to put on the tree. I had thought that perhaps we could use a few of the ornaments from the tree that was in the library, but the branches of my little sapling were much too fragile to support them. We decided to hang small paper plates that we decorated with drawings of snowmen, angels, and Santa. We cut holes in the plates and carefully strung them with yarn onto the branches. I then went outside and cut down some Bittersweet vine that had produced orange and red-orange berries, and took it back to the house where I draped the cutting around the tree like wreaths of garland. Our little tree had personality, that was for sure.

Christmas Eve was a wonderful, quiet evening. An order had arrived from Newtown Grocery that afternoon, and we dined on rotisserie chicken, liver pate, dried fruit, and crackers with orange marmalade. It was even better than our Thanksgiving feast. When I asked Mrs. Beale where our Christmas Eve dinner came from, she smiled at me and said, "Santa Claus." At Mrs. Beale's insistence, we sang Christmas carols well into the evening, including Mrs. Beale's favorite, "The Lord's Prayer," which she sang solo, of course. Around midnight we bid each other "Merry Christmas," and I made my way downstairs. It may not have been a Christmas Eve for most people, but for me it was exactly the type of Christmas I had always dreamed of ... with my own little family.

Winter held its grip well into April that year. We had spent much of that winter hunkered down in the mansion, only venturing outside when absolutely necessary. Bundled up in my cot, the cold Atlantic winds were so relentless that I would often wonder how these women had survived such conditions for so long. It seemed to me that only a boy—or a young body—could endure the winter nights. It amazed me that they had survived this long and it gave me even more respect for the incredible inner strength of these women. Whenever I asked Edie or Mrs. Beale about the past, specifically how they had survived such challenges, they brushed off the question with a laugh, or sometimes a song such as "Blue Skies" or "Life Is Just a Bowl of Cherries" (it took little prompting for "the great singer" and "the great dancer" to break into song). Mrs. Beale's attitude was to live in the present and to celebrate the gift of today. She was enamored of Dr. Norman Vincent Peale and his belief in the "power of positive thinking." I believe that this helped them survive the challenges of their lives. She and Edie would frequently listen to Dr. Peale's sermons on the radio, and Mrs. Beale was visibly moved by the experience, tears in her eyes. Their ability to not only accept their circumstances but to celebrate them was something I really did not fully appreciate until many years later, when I was an adult and life's events challenged my own strength and survival instinct. Looking back, the idea that they could live happily in these conditions astonishes me. But at the time, I confess, I didn't give much thought to it because I was so happy to be needed and to be a part of a loving family.

Spring arrived and with it the return of the Geddes estate staff. Charlotte was a sight for sore eyes, and I excitedly told her all about my adventures at Grey Gardens over the last few months. She seemed stunned that I had stuck it out and had survived the winter with the Beales. Now that that warmer days were at hand, my responsibilities at Grey Gardens grew exponentially, and it wasn't just the resumption of my gardening duties.

One of my tasks was to answer the telephone. Very often, days would pass without the phone ringing and when it did, I was always caught off-guard. Oddly, the call felt like an assault on our private world. Upon hearing the phone, Mrs. Beale would call out, "Edie! The telephone is ringing," after which Edie would call out from wherever she was: "Alright, I'll get it" and then do nothing. The phone would continue to ring, and the same exchange would echo through the house again, with Mrs. Beale calling out and Edie answering that she would get it but doing nothing. Eventually, after the third go-round of this exchange, and while the phone continued ringing, Edie would finally call out, "Jerry! Answer the telephone!" I would then drop whatever I was doing and race toward the phone. Soon I got accustomed to this ritual and would head toward the phone in anticipation of Edie's order to answer it. As it was usually either Newtown Grocers calling about a food order or Charlotte calling to speak to me about an issue at the Geddes mansion, it was never a big deal if the caller had hung up by the time I reached the phone. However, there was one day that spring when I made it to the phone in time to answer before the caller had hung up. And it was a phone call that would change my life, and the lives of the Beales as well.

At first I didn't understand what the man on the other end of the phone was saying. He told me that his name was David and that he was working with his brother and someone named "Lee." He wanted "permission" for something involving a film. Not really understanding what exactly he wanted, but knowing it was something that was beyond my scope of authority at the house, I called out to Edie to come to the phone. To my surprise, she was standing right next to me; perhaps she had heard me repeat the word *film* and quickly made her way downstairs to the phone. I handed it over to her and returned to my chores.

Though I didn't hear the rest of her conversation, I began to understand that something out of the ordinary had taken place. According to Edie, the caller was filmmaker David Maysles, and "Lee" was Mrs. Beale's niece Lee Radziwill. David and his brother, Albert, had been hired by Lee to make a film about her childhood, and he was calling to ask permission to visit the house to shoot some footage. They were also interested in having Mrs. Beale act as a narrator for this "home movie" that they were making; Lee obviously remembered Mrs. Beales wonderful recitative talents. What she couldn't have known was the current conditions under which her aunt and cousin now lived, otherwise I doubt she would never have put the filmmakers in touch with them.

To say that the request was met with excitement from Edie would be a vast overstatement. Despite her flamboyant performance for the camera in the film *Grey Gardens*, at this point the film was little more than a family movie for Lee—and Edie was not enthusiastic about the project. I am not sure if she was merely being protective of her mother, whether she was hesitant to reveal their living conditions, or whether there was some antipathy toward Lee, but she was definitely against the idea of Lee's film in the beginning. Still, David Maysles continued to call, and he assured Edie that the filming would only take one day, that they would cause as little disruption as possible. I had learned by now that subjects as mundane as ordering groceries could often lead to long and frustrating negotiations with Edie, so I could only imagine what this negotiation was like for David. Edie would vacillate with each conversation with David, alternately dismissive, then enthusiastic, then disinterested. Finally, after many conversations with him, permission was granted and a date was set for an initial visit.

I was too busy with my daily activities to pay much notice to the sudden activities in which Edie was engaged in preparation for the arrival of the visitors, most of which involved what she would wear when they arrived that week. She greeted them on the front porch wearing a dark skirt and sweater with a paisley bandana tied around her head; a very sedate choice for Edie, to be sure. David did most of the talking while his brother, Albert, stood silently in the background. They seemed pleasant enough, but upon meeting them in person, Edie really took a shine to them. David in particular caught her fancy, and her appreciation of this young and handsome man was visible in her expression from the moment they met.

A few more of these informal meetings took place over the next month, always between Edie and the brothers Maysles, always on the front porch. With each of these meetings, I noticed Edie's wardrobe becoming more and

more daring, and her behavior more and more coquettish.
I had no idea what exactly they were discussing, nor did it
occur to me to ask. Finally, the Maysles were invited *inside*
to meet Mrs. Beale, and it was then that I was introduced
to them as the caretaker of the house. David questioned
me about the electricity in the mansion, the conditions of
the rooms, and which outlets in the house were actually
working. (The answer was: very few.) Albert remained
quiet most of time the time, and I did my best to help
them navigate around the minefield of debris throughout
the house. I could see the astonishment in the eyes of the
Maysles, just as I had experienced on my first visit the year
before. Nevertheless, however overwhelmed they may
have been in this environment, they never once displayed
any sign of judgement or disgust. To their everlasting
credit, they remained composed and polite to Mrs. Beale,
Edie, and me.

Finally, the day of the actual filming arrived. The
Maysles arrived early that morning, camera in tow, along
with two additional people—a woman and a man who'd
come with them from Manhattan. The woman was Mrs.
Beale's niece, Lee Radziwill and the man was Peter Beard,
a noted photographer. It was Beard who suggested the
Maysles to Lee—and it was also he who would eventually
end up owning the footage of the "home movie" they
were shooting.

In addition to being Edie's cousin and Mrs. Beale's
niece, Lee was also the sister of Jacqueline Kennedy, a fact
that was not disclosed to me at the time. I thought when

I first saw her that she looked familiar, but I just assumed it was the family resemblance to Edie that I was seeing. I know it seems remarkable to say this now, but back then I honestly had no idea of Mrs. Beale's prestigious lineage, or that she was related to the former First Lady. Mrs. Beale would often express pride in her heritage, telling me grandly on more than one occasion, "I was born a Bouvier, *not* a Beale," but the meaning behind this comment was totally lost on me at the time. "Bouvier" meant no more to me than "Geddes," or any of the other well-known families that resided in East Hampton.

Although I was not privy to the conversation that occurred between Edie and Lee that morning, it was clear from the body language that it was not a joyous reunion for the cousins. Edie's mood seemed particularly tense, and it intensified as she conversed with Lee on the porch, raising her voice more than once. I was later to learn that the porch was as far as Lee was permitted to go; she was forbidden from entering the mansion—in fact, Edie didn't even want her on the porch, I was told later. It wasn't made clear to me why this edict was handed down, but knowing Edie, I think this was more an act of defiance against Lee than out of any concern she had about the state of the house. After all, Edie had no problems allowing the Maysles inside. Lee, however, was allowed to go to the first landing but no further. From my own dealings with Edie, I knew that it usually caused a person more frustration to question her about her motives than merely to accept them and move on. I am not sure that Lee was of this same mind, but after about ten minutes of intense exchanges—which I saw but did not hear—Lee retreated from the porch and back to the front yard where she stayed for the rest of the visit.

I was instructed by Edie to set up a folding table next to the old abandoned car and to serve refreshments to the guests. Mostly it was gimlets, which Mrs. Beale had instructed me how to make and which I frequently served to her. I mixed similar batches for our guests, but Lee never took one. Perhaps she didn't care for gimlets—or for the plastic tumblers in which I was serving them. Whatever the reason, she seemed as if she could use a drink; the distress on her face was clearly visible. Was it the harsh reception she received from Edie? Or was it the shock of the conditions in which she found her relatives living? I didn't ask, I just did as I was told. In addition to my bartending duties, I assisted David in setting up lamps on stands that led to the bedroom where Mrs. Beale presided, making sure that cords were securely taped down and that the working outlets were not overburdened.

For much of the filming, the cats—except for the ones that never left Mrs. Beale's bedside—remained out of sight, although their moaning and growling could be heard echoing throughout the house. Mrs. Beale was kind and gracious to the filmmakers; she asked the Maysles about their families—their mother especially—and how long they had been working in "moving pictures." At first, she didn't understand that the film they were shooting included sound, and once she found that out she seemed very pleased. At one point, she asked Edie where Lee was and Edie leaned over the bed and whispered something in her ear that ended the conversation. I have no idea what it was that Edie said, but the subject of Lee visiting her Aunt Edith was never broached again by Mrs. Beale. In fact, I didn't see Lee again after those first few moments outside on the front lawn. She and Peter seemed to disappear as quickly as they had arrived.

After about four or five hours of filming, the Maysles packed up their lamps and camera and left. I must admit that a part of me was relieved by their exit. Finally, after all these weeks of meetings and discussion, our lives could return to normal. I had no idea that the opposite was true—and that it was only the beginning.

The days that followed were relatively uneventful, but at the same time, I had the odd feeling that changes were on the horizon. Over at the Geddes mansion, Charlotte spoke of rumors that were circulating in town that a few elected officials had been alerted to the worsening conditions at the Beale's house. Though this was troubling to me, I never let on to Mrs. Beale or Edie that I had heard such things, as I feared that gossip may cause more harm than good by throwing the household into an unnecessary panic. But I did step up my efforts just in case. I felt that if the front yard was at least cleared out a bit, the neighbors might be a somewhat appeased, and back off on their complaints. This wasn't necessarily an easy thing, as the list of my chores at the house was ever growing. I soldiered on as best I could, attempting to create some sort of order out of the chaos.

Then, one hot June afternoon I had just left the Geddes estate for Grey Gardens when a team of fire trucks, EMTs, and police vehicles rushed by me in a frenzy of light and noise. I knew in my heart that there would be only one place they could be heading. I looked into the sky for any indication of smoke, but there was none. I felt a momentary relief, but then another thought crossed my mind. If there was no fire, what was going on? I quickly picked up the pace on my bike as I tore down West End Road.

When I arrived at the house, my stomach fell. There were county vehicles parked all along the northern section of the grounds, one of them labeled "Board of Health Suffolk County, NY." A fire truck had rolled onto the lawn and was parked close to the abandoned car. I quickly noted a fire hose leading to the front porch and my initial fear of fire once again popped into my head. I jumped off my bike and darted inside. The EMT workers had already made their way upstairs, and standing before me were some official-looking men dressed in dark suits. I ducked past them and made my way to Mrs. Beale's room, where a large, heavyset female worker towered over Mrs. Beale, who was visibly shaken by what was happening around her. She called out to me as soon as she saw me, and I ran over to her. I had never seen her in such an agitated state, and my anger turned to fury at this oversized harridan that was clearly frightening Mrs. Beale. She bellowed at Mrs. Beale that she had to come with her and vacate the house immediately. With the courage that only the ignorance of youth can muster, I shot back at her, "What do you think you're doing to her? Stop it!"

Then I saw Edie, standing behind the EMT woman, with a look of terror in her eyes. "Edie, what is going on?" I demanded. The woman said, "This house is uninhabitable. It is unsafe and unsanitary. They have to leave for their own good!"

"Wait a minute!" I shouted, noticing Edie's look of surprise at my boldness. She had never before seen me in such a forceful manner. Then again, neither had I. "You are scaring Mrs. Beale! Can't you see how upset she is?"

"This house is unsafe!" she reiterated, "It is in her best interest if this woman goes to a hospital!"

"This *woman*," I continued, "is *Mrs. Beale* to you! This is *her* home. She has broken no laws." At that time, a group of three men made their way into the room and over to Edie, where they handed her some papers. She reviewed them with a bewildered expression on her face. Meanwhile, one of the men brought a wheelchair into the room, which really set Mrs. Beale off. She grabbed ahold of the headboard with a look of terror, and this seemed to snap Edie to life finally.

"Don't bring that in here!" Edie cried out. "Stop right there!"

She began to scream at the workers to leave, and their exchange became quite heated. I stayed by Mrs. Beale's side, making sure I blocked the path between her and the man with the wheelchair. I had never seen Edie so infuriated. She had been testy with Lee a few weeks before, but there was a real fury in her face that frightened me. I think it frightened the EMT worker with the wheelchair, because he stopped dead in his tracks.

"This place is unfit for humans to live in," he spat at Edie. "There is dirt and filth all the way up to this room—cobwebs everywhere. How many cats do you have living here?"

"I'll clean it up!" Edie shouted. "I'll clean up downstairs, and I will start cleaning up these rooms. You cannot take us out of here. This is our house! I'll clean it up."

The exchange went on for several minutes, and I confess, the heat of the situation began to get to me and I began to break down a little. Edie was shouting, the EMT workers were shouting, Mrs. Beale was crying and clutching me so tight.

Finally, all grew silent. I looked over at the female worker, and she drew a deep breath and let it out.

"All right," she told Edie. "I will give you ten days. You have exactly ten days to get this place into some sort of livable state, you understand? This place is not only a health hazard for you and your mother, but it is a fire hazard for this entire neighborhood. You *must* do something about this filth and trash and all these cats, do you understand me?"

Edie nodded her head, obviously relieved and she quietly answered, "Yes. Thank you. I understand. We will have it cleaned up, I promise. I will call my brothers—they will help us. My cousin was just out here a few weeks ago, she will help as well. We will do it."

"Ten days!" the woman announced once more. "Ten days."

In the days following "the raid," as we began referring to it, I began to feel differently about my surroundings—my friends the Beales—and myself. I believe that the trauma of the event caused me to grow up a bit; whereas before I had thought of Mrs. Beale's house as a kind of surreal adventure, now I realized that the reality of the situation was quite different. It was a dangerous place. More than that, the safety and well-being of my Mrs. Beale—my "mother"—was in grave peril, not only by her surroundings but by the people of East Hampton. For the next week, my mantra became: "Ten days." I would repeat it over and over again. "Ten days."

Once the county workers left, I thought over the situation. What had Edie, and by extension, of course, myself, agreed to? It was a foregone conclusion on my part to assist in the massive cleanup, but how in the world were we to complete such a task? I was barely making a dent in clearing up the front yard the past week, and I had never seen Edie so much as pick up a broom the entire time I had known her. How were we going to accomplish such a task in ten days?

I began working that very night. The Board of Health had left Edie with a checklist of things that had to be done in order for the Beales to remain in residence, and number one on the list was the removal of all garbage. In this respect, my task was straightforward and I began there. Every day after I finished my chores at the Geddes estate, I would rush to the Beale's house carrying garbage bags—lots of them. Edie became not only cooperative in my efforts to clean, but encouraging. She immediately telephoned her girlhood friend Lois Wright, who recommended a local "jack-of-all" trades, Brooks Hyers, to help us in the cleanup. Edie also said that she was going to get in touch with Lee and Lee's sister, Jackie. Edie said, "After everything I've given up to her, the least Jackie can do is help out." I didn't know what she was referring to and I wasn't about to ask her at this point. There was too much to do, I just hoped that Edie would contact them as soon as possible. We needed all the help we could get. Bear in mind, the house that you see in the movie *Grey Gardens* is not the version that we set about cleaning. The house in the movie is actually the *cleaned-up* version, so you can imagine what we were up against!

That first night I began to shovel out the garbage in the kitchen, using a Tiffany lamp for illumination. The following day Brooks arrived, bringing black garbage bags and two helpers with him. They were nice, middle-aged black men, and though they jumped right in and began filling the enormous black garbage bags with debris, I wondered how long they would last. This was backbreaking work for men half their age, and the stench and heat alone could be overpowering. I could see in their faces utter amazement at the amount of sheer garbage we had before us. Still, they dove into the work without argument, although one of the men shook his head and turned to Brooks and said, "We're gonna need a lot more bags."

They worked on the kitchen, bagging up the wreckage, while I cleared the back staircase of the debris that Edie had swept down from the second floor. "This *awful* stuff!" Edie would mutter as garbage came careening down the stairs. "Awful! Awful!" We pressed on, discovering some astounding relics in the rubble—a solid silver chalice and a green marble Fabergé egg—as well as some very sad relics like skeletons of cats that appeared to have been deceased for many years. Apparently, these sick and dying cats would wander off to die alone. It was horrifying to find these, but we had little time to mourn the kitties and so pushed forward with the cleanup.

In the following days, I would bring armfuls of trash bags from the Geddes estate that I had used primarily for lawn clippings, fill them with garbage, tie them off with heavy metal ties, and pile them onto the bed of Brook's pick-up truck. Once the truck was filled to capacity, he would haul the bags away. Just where he was hauling them, I never asked. I simply focused on getting them out of the house. At times, I thought we were making good progress, because in certain rooms, such as the kitchen and dining room, I could actually see the wall on the opposite side of the room for the first time. We were able to clear away enough debris to get to the large picture- window in the dining room, which was thrilling. I excitedly reached up to pull the shade, only to have it crashing down on my head. Sunlight flooded the room, and after my vision adjusted to the light, I looked around to view the progress we had made. My joy was immediately deflated. The bright sunlight revealed the harsh reality of the task before us—there were still piles and piles of trash remaining and more dust and dirt than I had imagined. It was my understanding that Mrs. Beale had made arrangements to pay Brooks for his work, but I cannot imagine that it would compensate the enormous manpower the task of cleaning the house required. But deep down, I felt that Brooks was really unconcerned with how much money he was earning; like me, I sensed his real objective was in helping Mrs. Beale out of her predicament.

A few days after the raid, I was working inside the house when the phone rang. I made my way to the bedroom and knocked on the door, with Mrs. Beale giving me permission to enter. As I did, she turned to me and asked me to please answer the phone.

The voice on the other end said, "This is Feelin', who is this?" I stopped and looked at Mrs. Beale. After the events of the past few days, I assumed it was just another crank call and I quickly hung up the phone. A few moments later, the phone rang again.

"Hello," the caller said again. "This is Feelin' … Who is this?"

Again, I angrily hung up the phone. By this time, Edie had entered the bedroom asking who was calling. "Someone who keeps asking how we're feeling," I said. Then the phone rang a third time. I picked it up, but before I could say hello, the voice on the other end blurted out, "May I please speak to my sister!"

"Who is this?" I asked.

"This is Feelin'."

I don't know what came over me, but I suddenly blurted out, "Yeah? Well, I don't care how you're feelin', because we're not 'feelin' very well around here. We have no food … we have a mess to clean up—that's how we're feelin'!"

That remark brought Mrs. Beale to life. "It's my son! May I have the phone, please? It's *Phelan*."

Edie came over to me and took the phone. It was indeed Mrs. Beale's son, Phelan (pronounced "feelin'"). Though Edie had mentioned him before, this is the first time I had ever spoken with the man. I was dumbfounded and embarrassed by my blunder. I sneaked out of the room and back down to the first floor to continue my work. Needless to say, when I answered future phone calls from Phelan, I knew it was not a crank call.

After the phone call, I became privy to the exact nature of the Beale's financial situation and her son's involvement. For decades, the Beale's had survived on an inheritance from Mrs. Beale's father, Major John Bouvier. This had originally been controlled by Mrs. Beale's husband, Phelan Beale Sr., who doled it out in small monthly stipends to his ex-wife. After he died, Mrs. Beale's son, Phelan, Jr. took over the duties. This money barely covered food and utilities at Grey Gardens. In the event that more money was needed (for a household repair or some sort of maintenance), Edie would telephone Phelan, who would determine whether or not the situation was dire enough to advance additional funds. Over the years, of course, the Beales came to live with fewer and fewer of the "conveniences" of modern life, so that by the time I came to the house, they really were living on the bare essentials of food, telephone, partial electricity, gas, and plumbing. With the sudden matter of the Suffolk County Health Board in our faces, Edie was on the phone on a daily basis attempting to get more and more cash out of him and anyone else she could think of, to help fund the cleanup. I wanted to tell her that in addition to more money to hire more workers, we needed more *food*; ice cream and liver pâté can only sustain you for so long when you're performing backbreaking labor. She was in such a stressful state when she was talking to her brother, however, that I didn't attempt to relay this to her. I had another idea, and I turned to Charlotte for help. In her caring and thoughtful way, she would prepare substantial amounts of food, mostly sandwiches, and I would pack them in sacks and carry them back to the Beales. Some days I packed away as many as a dozen sandwiches to fuel myself, Brooks, and whomever else he was able to corral into helping us out.

It is in times of duress that our character is tested, and deep bonds between people are formed. I thought I couldn't have felt closer to Mrs. Beale and Edie than I already had, yet it was during these enormously stressful days that our bonds grew even stronger. Moreover, in the process of accomplishing the overwhelming task of cleaning up the house, I began to feel a sense of empowerment that I had never known. I grew to understand fully what it felt like to be responsible—not just for myself, but for another person. It was exhilarating—and exhausting.

One afternoon, about four days into the cleanup, I arrived at the Beales to find it once again a flurry of activity. People were combing all over the house like bees in a hive, carrying all sorts of bags and boxes out of the front door and throwing them into a large dump truck parked on the front lawn. At first, I froze, thinking that it was County workers evicting the Beales from their home and throwing away all their belongings, but then I noticed Edie on the porch talking calmly with one of the workers (a very handsome one at that ... typical Edie). I called out to her, and she pulled herself away from her conversation and came toward me. I noticed that she was wearing one of her "special" outfits: an opaque shower curtain cinched around her waist with the familiar blue bath mat tied around her head like a turban. Something out of the ordinary was happening, but apparently in a good way.

"Don't worry, Jerry. Everything is *fine!*" she said with a sweep of her hands. She then proceeded to explain to me that she had finally been able to get in touch with her cousin, and explain the nature of the situation at hand. Her cousin—or rather, her cousin's husband—had arranged for these men to help in the cleanup.

"Your cousin who was here at the house with those filmmakers?" I asked.

"Oh, no! Heavens no, not Lee! She's not married ... anymore," she replied with a wry smile. "Jackie. Lee's sister. Actually, it wasn't even Jackie who arranged all this. Mother talked to Mr. *Onassis.*"

I couldn't understand the name, but I really didn't care. Finally, someone other than Brooks and myself were there to tackle the cleanup. I quickly excused myself from Edie and ran up to check on Mrs. Beale, who was in a grand mood as well, surrounded by her kitties and serenading them with one of her old songs.

Less than a week left before the Board of Health returned, and the cleanup went into overdrive. With each passing day, more and more workers arrived to help us; by day six, I counted over two dozen! Edie was breathless with each new arrival, viewing each man, I suspect, as a knight in shining armor come to rescue her. Her charm and exuberance were overwhelming at times. She was in her element: dozens of strong, young men vying for her attention over one issue or another.

By the eighth day, an electrician showed up who asked to see the main fuse box that was located in the cellar of the house. Edie called out to me to please show the man to the basement, and I led the brave soul down into the depths. As we combed our way through the cobwebs of the basement, you could hear the creaking of the floor above and I said a silent "Our Father," hoping that the floor wouldn't collapse on us while we were beneath it. The feet of "Perfection," the enormous iron stove in the kitchen, were easily seen sticking through the floorboards above and we proceeded past them, flashlights in hand, sweeping away thick and dusty spider webs. He said, "We need to eliminate most of the electricity in the mansion," an odd statement, I thought, as I had no idea how that would be accomplished—or what we would do for electricity once he did. He assured me that he would fix it so that the rooms we used would remain powered, but in order to meet the health code, most of the electricity elsewhere would have to be shut off. "Whatever you need to do to meet the code," I said, relieved that professionals were there and taking care of things. Those last few days, every conceivable tradesman seemed to knock on the front door, each one busier and more concerned than the last with the amount of work they had to do in the short time frame.

Finally, time ran out. The inspectors from the Health Board arrived on schedule, as did our old "friends," the EMT workers. It had been ten labor-intensive days—and our own personal "Judgment Day" had arrived. We had done an amazing job. The house was a virtual shell. Gone were the towers of empty cat food cans that reached to the ceiling, as well as the piles of dusty, unidentifiable debris that clogged the stairway and landing. Holes in the walls and ceilings were patched, large plywood boards were hammered over windows with missing panes of glass, and tarps were hung up over warped doorways to further insulate the house from the elements. One group of workmen was busy hammering down new floorboards in the kitchen, another sweeping the stairway and hall, while a third was painting the new walls of the dining room baby blue—which I thought unattractive, but Edie approved. So much of the old furniture was rotted beyond repair that it was all discarded, leaving very few pieces. Gould's piano remained, as did valuable Tiffany lamps, but good old "Perfection" was hauled away to its final resting place. (It took nearly six men to carry that monster out of the kitchen.) In fact, the house was so empty that the slightest noise caused a loud echo that rang throughout the rooms. Anyone familiar with the film *Grey Gardens* will attest that there was still a very long way to go before the house would have been called attractive. But "attractive" was not what was required. The color of the walls didn't matter, nor did the lack of window coverings. It didn't matter whether the furnishings looked nice, or if they even existed. *Inhabitable*—that was the goal. That was the word that I repeated to myself over and over again as I watched the workers shuffle through the front door.

The Board of Health used a point system to determine the urgency of needed repairs, and they rated us on those repairs that were completed or were being addressed. At times, I followed the inspectors through the house as they made their notes and determined our future. Other times, the stress would be too much for me and I would retreat to the front porch, my self-designated "smoking area." Looking about the house at the now-cleared rooms, swept clean of debris, I stood proudly and witnessed as the board declared the conditions were in the "acceptable" range. Our ten days of hard work had paid off! An overwhelming sense of relief washed over me, then euphoria. Of course, some unacceptable conditions remained and much more work had to be done, but what we had accomplished met the minimum requirements of the Board of Health. Mrs. Beale and Edie were allowed remain in their residence!

As the inspectors got in their vehicles and drove off the property, I raced upstairs to Mrs. Beale to give her the joyous news. Oddly, the inspectors only entered one or two rooms on the second floor and never went onto the sunporch, where Mrs. Beale had sequestered herself upon their arrival. Just as I was about to shout the great news, Edie upstaged me by announcing the birth of a new litter of kittens. Believe it or not, this announcement, not the clearance by the Board of Health, became the "big" news of the day. Oh, well. Such was life at Grey Gardens.

Work continued after the Board of Health left, including repairing the collapsing eastern roof of the great house, some additional safety measures concerning the boiler in the basement, and the clearing of debris— *always* the clearing of debris. With continued help from the workers, however, I began to feel confident that we would be cleared of all the infractions, and I dug in with renewed energy.

Unfortunately, with the elation came the realization that many things had mysteriously gone missing from the house in recent days. Edie brought this to my attention. She talked of a built-in china cabinet located in a previously inaccessible area of the dining room that housed many of the Beale's valuables, including porcelain figurines and plates, Venetian glass goblets, and a Gorham silver service set. The cabinet had previously been hidden behind cascading mounds of empty cans and garbage, and the cleanup had revealed its existence—and, unfortunately, the valuables inside it. She then asked me if I knew what happened to the missing items and I assured Edie that I had no idea. Then it occurred to me: was she accusing me of stealing? The hired workers that we had never seen before, weren't they more likely suspects? Just a few days before, I had caught two of the workers stubbing out cigarettes on the dining room floor, and I had reprimanded them forcefully never to do something like that again as the threat of fire was ever present. This argument seemed to appease her suspicion for the moment, and we set about the processes of moving the most valuable items up into the attic where Edie stowed them away. (This was one of the very rare occasions in which I ventured into the attic, and only to the first landing. Edie made it clear to me early on that this was her private domain, which was fine by me since I had no desire to encounter any of the creatures that resided up there.) Of course, a few weeks later Edie would go looking for an item, forget where she had stored it, and the charges against me would begin all over again. I tried not to let it bother me, because I knew Mrs. Beale always dismissed such suspicions. Still, this happened again and again, no matter how many times I proved myself trustworthy.

For the most part, however, the weeks after we received the seal of approval from the Board of Health were really golden days. We still worked hard, but the pressure to work *fast* had been lifted. I allowed myself more than a few moments to step back and enjoy the feeling of accomplishment that accompanied a job well done. This usually happened at night, when Edie, Brooks, one or more of his friends, and I would relax on the front porch of the mansion at the end of a hard day's work. I would take a long drag on a cigarette, savoring the cool sensation of the smoke as I exhaled it into the warm summer wind. Whether it was a result of the stress of the deadline or the sheer physical exertion of the cleanup, Edie had lost weight and took great delight in showing off her new slim figure. Usually dressed in little more than a bathing suit or similarly skimpy outfit that showed off her legs, she would tell stories, sing, dance, and flirt—all the while relishing the undivided attention of us men. I don't recall ever seeing her as happy and engaging as she was on those summer evenings. For my part, I found myself cherishing the closeness I felt with my companions as our shared laughter and singing rang into the night. But honestly, the sweetest sound to me was that of the front door closing at bedtime; the boom of its great brass latch closing as it echoed through the empty rooms of the first floor. The sound had a feeling of grandeur, of greatness, of a great house beginning to reclaim its history. I was proud to be a part of that.

One day in late summer, I was summoned into the bedroom by Edie and Mrs. Beale for a discussion. I loved these times, when just the three of us spent hours together. This time, however, something felt different. As soon as I walked in the room, I could sense tension. Edie was in a highly-excited state, pacing and wringing her hands. I'd learned that this usually happened when she was at odds with Mrs. Beale on a subject—or person. Since I was, on occasion, the source of the conflict, I wondered if I was about to be upbraided.

"Come in, Jerry," Mrs. Beale said and motioned to me to sit next to her on the bed. She held one of her favorite kitties in her lap and slowly stroked its back

"What is it?" I asked her as I sat down slowly so as to not disturb the kitty.

"The Maysles want to come back and film again," Edie said, continuing to pace.

Mrs. Beale reached toward me and placed her hand on my arm. "How does that sound to you, Little Jerry?" she asked.

I had to stop and think. The Maysles? I really didn't know what they were talking about. Then I remembered the two men who had been at the mansion with Edie's cousin Lee all those months ago. So much had happened since then that I had completely forgotten about them. Was this for more footage for Lee's home movie? But Edie had said that Lee had told her she had decided to abandon the film. I asked if Lee had changed her mind, and Edie told me that this new film did not involve Lee. The Maysles wanted to come back to make their own film; a film entirely about the Beales and Grey Gardens.

I didn't know what to say. It was never my place to express approval or disapproval of anything that happened at their house. I respected Mrs. Beale too much to ever do that. But I was moved that she was asking my opinion about it; something that Edie seemed slightly perturbed about.

"Well," I said cautiously, not knowing exactly what the Beale's thoughts were, "I guess it sounds like a good idea if you like it. Could we make any money from it?"

This stirred up Edie. "Yes, we can make money from it! They want to come back here and film Mother and me on our own—nothing to do with Lee!" she exclaimed excitedly. "Or *Jackie*! It's about *us*."

Mrs. Beale sat watching Edie and smiled slightly, apparently enjoying her enthusiasm. She then looked over at me and shook her head knowingly. I smiled too. I knew what she was communicating. Edie was not about to let the opportunity to be in the spotlight pass her by, not at this late point in her life, and Mrs. Beale knew it. I offered that if Mrs. Beale and Edie agreed that it was a good idea, then I would be happy to go along with whatever they wanted. I was so immature and naïve about subjects like this, I had no other opinion to offer. If Mother thought it was good, then we should go ahead with it.

A week or so later, I was hacking away at a thick wisteria branch that was entangled around and threatening to bring down one of the few rain gutters that was still operational, when I looked up to see a white van stop in front of the house. The doors opened and two men—the same ones I recognized as having been with Lee those months before—exited and began to approach the house. One had a camera in his hand and the other had a small white box wrapped around his waist and carrying what looked like a microphone on a long stick. Suddenly, I heard Edie's excited voice echoing inside the house.

"It's the Maysles!" she exclaimed. "The Maysles are here!"

And with those few words, Edie, unknowingly, announced the beginning of the end of our private world at Grey Gardens.

CHAPTER FOUR: CAMERAS IN THE GARDEN

When Albert and David Maysles arrived at Grey Gardens that summer of 1973, it was just another work day for me. I stayed out of it all, since this was to be a film about the Beales, not me. The conversation between the three of us in the bedroom was the last I had heard of the project until the Maysles showed up a week later to begin filming. I did think that Mrs. Beale and Edie would be wonderful in a film, though—I had expressed this idea to Mrs. Beale long before Lee and the Maysles had ever shown up. "You're very interesting," I told her once. "Edie as well. The mansion. The estate. Someone should write about this or film it." Mrs. Beale chuckled at the notion, finding my suggestion amusing. And now, here the Maysles were, doing just that, although I don't think any of us had an idea what they had in mind for the finished film.

There didn't seem to be any sort of plan or guideline for what they were going to film—they simply filmed everything. I am not sure if they discussed with Edie what sort of film they envisioned. I do know that Edie told the Maysles on several occasions that she was hoping for a musical, while Mrs. Beale seemed totally disinterested. She liked David and Albert to be sure, and she enjoyed the moments when she was able to perform one of her old songs, but on the whole, she looked on the endeavor as a silly indulgence for Edie. None of us could have imagined the impact the final result would have on the world or our lives.

Upon hearing Edie's greet the Maysles, I crept around from the side of the house to the library, where I could peer out the window unobserved. Edie greeted them in "full gear" as Mrs. Beale called it. She was wearing a navy turtleneck sweater and a pair of shorts covered by a skirt that was turned upside down and pinned together with safety pins. She wrapped a sweater around her head that she fastened at the chin with a gold broach (an old Bouvier family heirloom). Of course, I had seen her in much more "eccentric" costumes than this one (the shower curtain dress and chef's apron that she had worn on her head when I first met her comes to mind), but this costume was destined to go down in history as her "revolutionary costume," based primarily on Edie's remarks to the Maysles that it was much too avant-garde for the conservative tastes of East Hampton.

As Edie conversed with the Maysles, I returned to work only to be summoned by her a few moments later. I hesitantly made my way, hoping that they weren't filming me as I approached. Really, I had no desire whatsoever to be on camera. I was very self-conscious about my appearance, particularly my teenage acne, and felt tongue-tied whenever the attention was focused on me. Happily, the Maysles had taken a break to re-load the camera while we made our re-introductions.

David once again asked for assistance in finding the best outlets in which they could plug in the lighting and sound apparatus. Knowing that the house had recently been re-wired and that only a few rooms had working outlets, I spent the better part of the day helping David set up lights. He placed a few tripods holding round silver lamps in the upstairs bedroom and down the hallway. From these tripods ran spools of extension cord that were strapped down along the floorboards with masking tape, and then ran to the few working outlets in the house. Nervous as I was about the stress these lights may be putting on the new wiring, it was nice to be acknowledged and asked to help out, something that I now recognize as a deliberate gesture by David to put me at ease. By the end of the day, I was excited to be a part of this new adventure—not to mention exhausted from all the work. My back was killing me! So, this was the glamour of show business?

Over the next few weeks, David and Albert recorded every moment at Grey Gardens. At first it seemed odd to arrive at the house and find the Maysles on the porch filming Edie, or setting up a shot in the bedroom with Mrs. Beale, but David and Albert were such kind and gentle people that it was difficult not to like them and welcome their presence. Also, I could understand their fascination with Mrs. Beale and Edie, and it was wonderful to see my friends receive such positive affirmation after all the problems they had faced over the past year. What truly amazed me, however, was how easily Edie and Mrs. Beale fell into it all; you would have thought they had been filmed at Grey Gardens their entire lives. Perhaps being members of an esteemed family had something to do with this. In a way, they were raised to be on display; they were taught how to behave in social situations and how to deal graciously with the attentions and interests of others.

Which leads me to an important point. People have often asked me if the film was really accurate. Did Edie and Mrs. Beale *really* behave that outlandishly when the cameras weren't rolling? My answer has always been, "ABSOLUTELY—YES!" Mrs. Beale and Edie were entirely themselves throughout the filming. The conversations, the sudden bursts of song, the arguments and the recriminations were all real, nothing was staged or enhanced for the sake of the cameras. Edie was *definitely* aware of the cameras, and her emotions may have been a bit heightened knowing that she was being filmed, but the basic honesty of the situations that were shot over the next three weeks were very real and routine. To me, the only difference was that Edie and Mrs. Beale now had an audience of three—and a camera—to play to.

That camera was almost a part of Albert, or vice versa, because he hardly ever stepped out from behind it. I remember thinking at the time that it was so light and portable that it looked like it could be used in a battlefield—and in a way, it was. Life at Grey Gardens was a battlefield of wills, egos, and emotions. I often wondered how difficult it must have been for Edie, a middle-aged woman with her own ideas and desires, to live according to her mother's rules and dictates. Often Edie would attempt to assert her opinion on a subject, and Mrs. Beale would cut her off dismissively without further argument. "You can't have freedom when you're being supported," Mrs. Beale comments to Edie in the movie, and that was pretty much the rule at Grey Gardens. It was Mrs. Beale's house, and in most instances what she said was the way it was going to be. That didn't mean, however, that Edie didn't push the limits to see how far she could go to get her way.

A good example of this is the photo album scene in the movie, in which Edie and Mrs. Beale are showing the Maysles some Beale family photos. The minute Edie dragged out the photos, I could feel the air thicken with tension. Mrs. Beale immediately made it known that there were some photos she did not want to be shared on camera, but it was obvious that Edie *did* want to share them and she was on a mission to have her way. It ended in a literal tug of war over a photo of Mrs. Beale as a young woman that was torn in the process. I never understood why some things worked up Edie into a state while others barely fazed her. There was just no predicting her response.

Another instance in which tempers flared between Edie and Mrs. Beale was in the upstairs sunroom. (The scene happens late in the film, but actually occurred early in the filming.) This time, it was Mrs. Beale who became argumentative when Edie refused to stop singing a song that Mrs. Beale disliked. I wasn't there to see this particular episode, but I certainly heard about it later that day from Mrs. Beale, who was still upset at Edie's behavior. As I said, these types of arguments happened frequently between the two women, so it wasn't an unusual occurrence. What *was* different was that Edie seemed to react bigger and prolong arguments for the sake of Albert and David—and the camera, of course. Let me say that I was never aware of the Maysles ever egging Edie on or attempting to aggravate a situation to heighten its drama for filming. I think that after so many years of having to keep her own counsel, Edie was overjoyed to have the opportunity to vent her frustrations in such a public forum. She felt that her obligation to care for her mother had robbed her of realizing her true potential in life and this film became the perfect opportunity to release her feelings of anger and frustration—so much so that I think she often went overboard in her desire to express them and losing all sense of perspective and proportion.

A well-known example of this behavior in the movie is when Edie rages at Albert for asking about one of Mrs. Beale's former companions, Tom Logan. The evening began pleasantly enough, with the Maysles filming the Beales in the main bedroom. Mrs. Beale began reminiscing about Tom, and Albert quite innocently asked her a question about their relationship. Suddenly, Edie began screaming at Albert. Edie at full-tilt anger could be a frightening sight, especially when it was directed at you, but to their credit, the Maysles remained calm and continued shooting until Edie's emotional storm subsided. It was this case throughout the filming; they simply shot events as they happened without any guidance or instigation on their end. Life at Grey Gardens was full of drama without anyone's help or prompting.

All during this time, I helped out when I was asked, but mostly I kept my head down and stayed out of the way. But I *was* captured on film one night when David and Albert joined one of our evening gatherings on the front porch, a frequent happening in the summertime when the heat inside the house got too unbearable. Edie was particularly distressed that night by the fleas. As hot as it was, wearing shorts was asking for trouble since the fleas would instantly attack your bare legs. I tried strapping flea collars to my ankles (a trick I suggested to the Maysles, who soon utilized it), but flea collars were only effective for so long and I hated the smell of the strong pesticide lotions that you had to rub on your legs. Edie, however, would have none of this—particularly with the Maysles and their camera around. She paraded about showing off her still shapely legs (she wasn't nicknamed "Body Beautiful Beale" in her youth for nothing), but at the same time making herself a prime target for flea attacks. By the end of the summer, her legs were battle-scarred from bug bites.

The Maysles themselves were an interesting contrast

to the Beales in terms of family relations. Unlike Edie and Mrs. Beale, they never raised their voices at each other or even had a disagreement or a conflict that I can remember. Albert was always behind that camera and rarely spoke to anyone other than a "good morning" or "how are you today?" greeting. David was really the front man of the operation. He interacted the most with us all and he was definitely the focus of Edie's attention throughout the shoot. Yet, being Edie, there were some days she would completely ignore David and focus her attentions on Albert, suggesting that he was the man that she was destined to marry and that they should run away together to the south of France or Brazil. Even from behind the camera, I could see Albert blush at Edie's flirtations, but he never lost focus and never turned the camera away from her.

The Maysles arrived every morning from a house in East Hampton in a white Volkswagen van in which they kept their film and recording equipment. I never really understood how it all worked. I just knew that they moved around the mansion with ease and precision. As with their first visit at Grey Gardens, I never witnessed either one flinch or pass judgement on anything they encountered while at the house. They were gentlemen to us all in every sense of the word. As filming progressed, they developed a clear fondness for the Beales. I then began to have affection for David and Albert. Being little more than a child myself, I looked up to them as role models of sorts; the kind of men that I wished my father and brothers could have been.

The Maysles didn't come every day; in fact, I was never really sure when they were going to be there and when they weren't. I didn't think to ask what the schedule was—it wasn't my place—but Edie would often talk to me at the end of a day's shoot about the Maysles and how wonderful it was that they were doing this for her. She truly felt that the film was her chance at stardom. Not only was this her destiny, she believed, but it was her turn to grab the limelight away from her cousin Jackie, whom she felt had unjustly upstaged her in life. She was determined to take this opportunity to right that situation. I hesitated to mention to her that the Maysles were actually filming us *all*; Mrs. Beale, Brooks, Lois, me—we were all involved. It wouldn't have mattered. To Edie, this was her moment. We were all merely her supporting cast.

Today with the gift of hindsight, I realize, too, that Edie must have also felt a certain degree of desperation at this time at the passing of her youth. She was, when the filming began, fifty-six years old, only four years away from age sixty, and, in her mind, old age. Now that I have passed that milestone myself, I can understand the certain amount of desperation she must have felt at her life seeming to pass her by and this movie being her final chance to attain the dreams of her youth. To someone who still clung tenaciously onto her identity as a debutante, this realization had to feel devastating to her. As she says to the Maysles at one point in the film, "You don't see me as I see myself ... I see myself as a young girl." I think that was probably the most touching—and honest—thing I ever heard her say.

Since the Health Department raid, we had no shortage of curiosity seekers who would suddenly appear on the front lawn at all hours of the day and night. Many of them were residents of East Hampton who had obviously read the news accounts of the situation and just wanted a glimpse of the house to see if it was as bad as they'd read. Visitors usually rushed off after they saw me—a few lingered until I asked them to leave the property. Few were real trouble makers, although we did find evidence of vandalism once or twice that Edie blamed on some teenage "hoodlums" that she had seen skulking about. Having grown up on the mean streets of Brooklyn, I wondered just what an East Hampton "hoodlum" looked like. Juvenile delinquents in Docksiders and polo shirts? Still, with all the publicity over the past few months, I grew increasingly vigilant to any out of the ordinary happenings around the perimeter of the grounds. But even I had no idea just how "out of the ordinary" things would get one late September day.

It took place, ironically, on a day when the Maysles were not at the house filming. I was enjoying a break on the front porch, smoking, when I noticed a large gold sedan stop in front of the house. I watched as a woman got out of the rear of the car. She was tall and had on large, round sunglasses with a multi-colored scarf wrapped around her head. As she approached the house, I stamped out my cigarette and walked over to greet her. Even at a distance, I could tell that this woman—obviously, someone of means, judging by the car and the fact that she had a driver—looked familiar. Actually, she looked startlingly like Edie. Then it suddenly dawned on me: this was Jacqueline Kennedy Onassis!

Here at Grey Gardens?

I had been a child when the nuns in our classroom had us kneel beside our desks to pray for President Kennedy when he was killed, and it was something that I had never forgotten. Now, here was Mrs. Kennedy herself, a woman whose image in mourning was etched into the nation's memory forever, stepping around and over the weeds and crabgrass that covered the front lawn. Just as she came within a few feet of me and before I could offer a greeting, a window was slammed open upstairs above us. Leaning out the window, Edie yelled, "Don't let her in! Don't you *dare* let her in!" I was dumbfounded. I had barely recovered from the shock of seeing the former First Lady, and now Edie was forbidding her from entering the house. I wasn't sure what to do or how to handle this situation. I mean, this was *Jacqueline Kennedy Onassis!* I stood there speechless, wanting to apologize for Edie's ranting but not knowing where to begin. I turned to Mrs. Onassis, who was now standing right in front of me and looking elegant in a dark brown pantsuit and paisley top beneath a belted jacket. By comparison, I looked like a dirt bomb in my paint-stained *Newsday* sweatshirt, filthy blue jeans, and painters cap. I suddenly felt very self-conscious and embarrassed, which was nothing new. Before I could apologize for my appearance, however, she extended a hand.

"You must be Jerry," she said warmly, shaking my

hand. "I've heard a lot about you. My aunt has grown very fond of you, I'm told."

Her aunt? Mrs. Beale was Jacqueline Kennedy Onassis's aunt?

As I said before, I had no idea up until this point exactly whom the Beale's were or to whom they may be related. To me, they were just people who were in dire straits and in need of help. I knew that they were of a distinct lineage, and I was certainly impressed with Lee when she came out to visit, but I had no idea that Lee's sister and the "Jackie" that Edie often talked about was *that* Jackie. I was still just a kid, really, in my experience and knowledge—and a very sheltered kid at that. When your primary objective as a child is simply to survive your surroundings and make it to the next day, your world view becomes very narrow.

"You *are* Jerry, aren't you?" she asked as she removed her sunglasses. Her voice was light and smooth—that familiar dialect that we had all heard when she was First Lady.

"Yes, I am," I managed to mumble. "I'm friends with Mrs. Beale and Edie."

"I am happy to meet you," she said as she smiled at me. She then looked up toward the window where Edie had been screaming at us. As if on cue, Edie slammed the window shut. I watched her surprised expression as her eyes wandered across the front of the house and around the property. I can only describe this expression as one of disbelief—shock, actually. Perhaps she had once known this place in much better days and in a much different state. Who knew when she had last been here, but the look on her face told me it had to have been a very long time ago.

Finally, she said, "My aunt trusts you, Jerry. It seems you have been adopted."

"Yes," I said, wondering how she knew so much about me, "I am very fond of Mrs. Beale and Edie. I am trying my best to help them out. We had some problems with the Board of Health a few weeks ago, but that's all been taken care of."

She smiled and nodded as she began to walk around the side of the house. Her response—or lack of it—seemed odd to me, but then I remembered my conversation with Edie the day when all the workers showed up. She had told me then that her cousin had made the arrangements for the help with the cleanup. It finally dawned on me. That cousin was Jacqueline Kennedy Onassis!

"How on earth were you ever invited inside the house?" she asked in a puzzled tone.

"Oh, well, you see, I work just down the road on Lily Pond Lane for Mr. Gerald Geddes. I am his assistant gardener."

"Mr. Geddes?" she asked, turning to look at me.

"Yes, Mr. Gerald Geddes."

"I see," she said, and I detected a slight smile on her face.

Just then, Edie appeared at the back door. I could tell by the look on her face that it was not to welcome us. "Jerry, I don't want her coming into the house," she said again, her arms folded across her chest and looking directly at Mrs. Onassis.

"Hello, Edie," Mrs. Onassis said as she approached the back door. "I just wanted to stop in and see how things were going out here. How is Aunt Edith?"

They now stood a few feet apart from each other in silence. I felt it would be best if I backed off and gave them some privacy, so I stepped away.

Although I couldn't hear their conversation, this was clearly a tense exchange, much in the manner she had spoken to Lee. After a few moments, Mrs. Beale began calling out from the upstairs bedroom. Mrs. Onassis reached past Edie toward the door as if she were going to enter the house, but Edie blocked her. I couldn't believe how Edie was behaving. Mrs. Onassis had saved us from the Health Department after all. But then again, nothing that Edie did surprised me.

Mrs. Onassis turned away and began to walk back to her car. She was holding a handkerchief up to her mouth and nose as she made her way along the path. I quickly dropped what I was doing and followed her. I wasn't sure if she was upset from the exchange with Edie, or if the smell of the house had suddenly overwhelmed her, but she was quickly retreating. I felt that someone should acknowledge what she did and how much help she had provided in the cleanup.

As I caught up to her, she turned and said "Jerry, I need your assistance. I have some men coming in the next few days to look over some of the repairs. I wonder if you would be so kind as to make sure they are allowed into the house."

"Of course," I responded. "Thank you so much for all you've done for the Beales."

She smiled. "Also, I will be sending some things for my aunt and for Edie. Some household items—will you make sure they get them?"

"Yes, of course."

"Thank you," she said and then continued toward the car. Her driver opened the door for her and as she got inside, she looked back at the house one last time. I can't imagine what she must have been thinking. Within a few seconds, she was gone.

A few days later a package arrived for the Beales that included some blankets, a pair of heavy rain boots, some crackers and *pâté*, a bottle of Beefeater's gin (Mrs. Beale's favorite), some dresses and sweaters, and a few other odds and ends. For her part, Edie never acknowledged her cousin's visit or the "care package" that she had sent—except when she used one of the blankets to try to extinguish a fire that had erupted in the upstairs hallway a few weeks later. After the fire was safely put out by David Maysles, she remarked dismissively that the blanket hadn't been any help at all in smothering the flames.

Although I was used to Edie's mercurial nature, Albert and David were still new to her sudden and dramatic mood shifts. I had grown accustomed to being locked out of the house on a regular basis by Edie, but when the Maysles were locked out of the house for an entire week, they were at a loss. "What is going on here, Jerry?" Albert asked me when I rode up to the house to find them stranded on the front lawn. "How often does she do this sort of thing?"

I laughed. "Every other week or so, although she hasn't done it in a while. You've been lucky. You just have to go along with it."

"What should we do? Is there any way to get inside?" Albert asked.

"Well, sometimes I call out to Mrs. Beale and if she hears me, she will tell Edie to let me in." So, I began calling out her name, and soon David and Albert joined in. It was actually a funny scene, like three naughty little boys being punished and calling out to be let back in. But it was to no avail; Mrs. Beale never answered back.

I had plenty of tasks to keep me busy working around the yard, but the Maysles didn't know what to do. They were about to leave when Edie suddenly appeared in an upstairs window and told them that they couldn't come in that day. She gave no reason as to why, that was just the way it was going to be. So they filmed conversations with Edie from the lawn as she stayed at the upstairs window (this sequence appears in *The Beales of Grey Gardens*, the documentary follow-up that utilizes footage not used in *Grey Gardens*). She gave her views on everything from the current election in East Hampton, to the Republican Party, to her uncertainty about the Maysles naming the film *Grey Gardens* because she was afraid people would think it was a film about flowers.

The Maysles left after a few hours, and were gone for the rest of the week. A few days later they were back and everything was again normal again. Edie was her old vivacious self, dancing around the Maysles singing "You Ought to Be in Pictures" and telling Albert that they should run off together. Throughout it all, the Maysles remained calm and unfazed. In fact, the more eccentric her behavior, the more they seemed to enjoy it—and, of course, it was *all* captured on film.

Edie wanted more and more singing and dancing in the film. After she serenaded the Maysles, her idea of doing a full-out musical number came up. "I do terrific dances," she said to David. "And, Mother was a great singer. She had marvelous salons here in the summertime when I was a little girl. Dozens and dozens of people would come to hear her sing." David and Albert looked at each other in bemusement and then David suggested that Edie rehearse and perform a musical number for the camera. And not just the spontaneous bits that she had done thus far but a choreographed musical number. "Do whatever you want to do, Edie," David told her with a big smile. Well, she was beside herself with joy. "Oh, marvelous!" she exclaimed. "I've got to decide what I'm going to do *right now*. It's got to be carefully planned out." It was a delight to see her enthusiasm blossom, rehearsing various musical numbers well into the night.

Usually after the Maysles finished filming for the day, Edie would scamper about the house selecting her wardrobe for the next day's shoot, laying her choices over the second-floor banister while she matched pieces. After much consternation about what song to sing and what outfit to wear, she decided on "The VMI [Virginia Military Institute] Marching Song," which was certainly not a choice I would have expected. But Edie was very fond of the march and had a recording of it that she could rehearse to, which may have been the reason for her choice, although the finished routine looked more like an improvised dance than a choreographed number. But that was Edie. Mrs. Beale was content to have a few of her old recordings played on the record player, singing along with her younger self for a few verses. She seemed even more enthusiastic about reciting some of her favorite verse, including "Lorraine, Lorraine, Lorree," a poem by Charles Kingsley about the murder of a young mother, which always moved her to tears.

It was about this time that I obtained a washing machine for Edie and Mrs. Beale. The Geddes estate had purchased a new one for the house, and I was given the job of getting rid of the old one. I felt it was a windfall, and that the Beales could certainly use it. Up until then, they had used an old-fashioned washing machine with a wringer attached that most likely dated back to '40s; it was used by Edie only when absolutely necessary, and very ineffectually at that. This was one of the reasons for Edie's eccentric wardrobe; it was easier to grab a drape from the window and wrap it around herself than to wash a dress by hand. Since Mrs. Beale rarely left the confines of the bedroom or the upstairs porch, she usually dressed in loose bathing suits or, in the winter, layers of sweaters and coats. I felt that the Geddes's washing machine would not only be a big help but may score some points with the Board of Health. I often wondered if Mr. Geddes was aware of my friendship with the Beales and had guessed that I would give the washer to them, thus his directive for me to take it.

I moved the washing machine to Grey Gardens by rolling it down Lily Pond Lane from the Geddes house. (Sometime later, Edie's friend Lois Wright told me that my wheeling of the washing machine down the street was looked upon with disapproval by the neighbors, but I didn't care.) Despite my best intentions, however, it turned out that my idea of giving them a washing machine was of little consequence. Mrs. Beale didn't know how to use a washing machine and wasn't about to venture down the stairs to use it. Edie not only ignored it, she appeared outright irritated that I had brought it to the house. I had no idea how she truly felt until I saw the moment in *Grey Gardens* when Edie says that my gesture was a covert action on my part to "seal the deal," as she put it, of my status as a permanent resident in their home. No good deed goes unpunished, as they say, and my great idea ended up being a big waste of time and energy. For the most part, the washing machine stood unused in the kitchen.

With news of the filming now attracting local attention, the telephone rang more frequently. It was usually crank-calls or busybodies from the village wanting to know about the movie. But occasionally the phone would ring and I would pick it up only to be greeted by a deep male voice with a thick accent asking to speak with Mrs. Beale. After a few phone calls, I found out the voice belonged to none other than Aristotle Onassis! At first, he called to check on the workmen, but by this time most of the essential repairs had been completed and the workmen were long gone (there was, however, still plenty of work for myself, and occasionally for Brooks, to attend to.) But Mr. Onassis continued to telephone just to talk to Mrs. Beale. I later read that Mr. Onassis had lost his son in a plane crash, and I believe that he found talking to Mrs. Beale a form of comfort and consolation for his grief. I know it surprises people when I say this, considering the situation that she found herself living in, but Mrs. Beale possessed a great wisdom about life and living. I always turned to her for advice if I were in a situation in which I was confused about what action to take, or if I were feeling sad and lonely. She always left me feeling better. I suspect that Mr. Onassis discovered this to be true as well. For her part, Mrs. Beale—still flirtatious at seventy-seven—enjoyed teasing Mr. Onassis that she knew he "liked singers." I didn't understand this remark at the time, but I came to realize it was a reference to his former lover, the famed opera singer Maria Callas. Usually a day or so after a phone call from Mr. Onassis, a large care package would arrive for us at the house, stuffed with all sorts of food, goodies, and gifts. Mr. Onassis, perhaps even more than his wife, was responsible for saving us from eviction that summer—arranging for the workmen, paying for the repairs, checking to make sure all was going well. He continued to help Mrs. Beale and Edie financially until Mrs. Beale's death.

By the time of the washing machine incident, the Maysles had been filming at Grey Gardens for over a month. Although I was on hand most every day to watch, it was hard to get a grasp on exactly what the finished project would look like. Edie acting out and saying outrageous things was hardly new to me, but I wondered what strangers would think seeing this outrageous character for the first time. Would they laugh with her or at her? The thought of anyone laughing at Mrs. Beale broke my heart. How would anyone know by just watching a movie what a wonderful person she was? As good as the movie might be, how could it convey all the love that she had inside? I worried that people might think she was just a loony old woman. Also, and perhaps this is difficult to believe, but what the Maysles were filming felt to me to be just normal day to day life at Grey Gardens. There was no major event like the Health Department raid or even Jacqueline Kennedy's visit to make the movie dramatic. It was just Mrs. Beale, Edie, and occasionally me and a few others doing what we did every day. What on earth would people find so fascinating about *that*?

As autumn arrived, Albert and David's visits became less frequent. But there was one important event that they wanted to film, and they needed my help in doing so. On October 5, Mrs. Beale was turning seventy-eight years old, and the brothers wanted to film a birthday party sequence to take place in the downstairs dining room. It was one of the first rooms to be cleaned up, and it remained in fairly good condition. Once filled to the rafters with garbage, it was now clean but virtually empty except for a few pieces of furniture. It was never intended to be a surprise party for two reasons: one, Mrs. Beale was as sharp as a tack, and she would have quickly detected any attempts at deception, and two, having the party in the dining room meant we would have to get her downstairs, which was someplace she rarely went. She was comfortable moving about the second floor, but that was about the extent of it. Getting her down the flight of stairs and back up again required some planning. In fact, the only sequence in the entire film that you could say was "set up" was the birthday party. The night before, we made sure the stairs were swept and the shades in the dining room were cleaned and opened to allow as much light in as possible. Since the bittersweet vines covering the windows allowed very little light inside the room, I set up lamps in the vestibule to give additional illumination. We set the dining room table for a party of five: Mrs. Beale, Edie, Lois Wright, and Mrs. Beale's friend Jack Halmuth—a man I had never met before and would never see again—and me. As the party approached, however, I began to feel that I really didn't care to be on camera. I was never comfortable during those few times when the camera was on me; it made me feel extremely ill at ease and self-conscious. I was much more of a "behind the scenes" person, and I felt much more comfortable staying in the background and helping

David and Albert. So, when filming the party began, I stayed out of camera shot.

Edie had obtained a cake from some friends of Mrs. Beale and ordered a particular brand of wine to be served that was not available at Newtown Grocers but had to be special ordered. Just before the party, she had sent me to pick up the wine, which was a bit ridiculous because at age seventeen I was clearly underage. This thought, of course, wouldn't have occurred to her, and I somehow convinced the store to go along and let me buy it. All during the party, Mrs. Beale was, as always, gracious to everyone—especially to Edie's friend Lois, whose birthday present to Mrs. Beale was a small blank notebook. I thought this was a very odd gift indeed, as she had no use for a little notebook, but if Mrs. Beale thought so too, it never showed. She was as effusive over the notebook as if it had been a diamond necklace. I also remember Mr. Helmuth's stunned expression when he first entered the house and looked around. Though he was a friend of the family, it was obvious he had not been inside the house for years and was not prepared for what he saw. But despite the surroundings, he also remained polite and charming throughout the evening.

Edie did her best to play hostess, even though I could tell she was anxious about having guests over. She seemed particularly uneasy about having Lois there, no matter that she was a frequent visitor to Grey Gardens and one of the few people allowed upstairs to visit Mrs. Beale. She and Edie had been friends since they were girls, but it was a complex friendship. Edie felt a rivalry with Lois for Mrs. Beale's affections, as Lois had lost her mother when she was a young girl and looked on Mrs. Beale as a surrogate mother. Edie felt threatened by this—much as she did about my relationship with Mrs. Beale—and sometimes her feelings erupted and she caused a scene. I remember her being very short with Lois that evening, especially when Lois offered to help Edie serve the birthday cake. Mrs. Beale didn't help the situation by criticizing Edie's hostess skills ("She's no waitress, I'll tell you that," she remarked), but Edie managed the party without spilling any drinks. I enjoyed staying back and watching the party unfold without the pressure of being on-camera.

After "Happy Birthday" was sung to Mrs. Beale and the cake was passed around, the party began to wind down. Lois and Mr. Helmuth took their leave, and Albert and David and I began to disassemble the lights and cables. A silence had fallen over the house that had only a few hours before been bustling with energy and activity. After saying good night to Albert and David, Edie and I got Mrs. Beale upstairs to her room. She was quite tired from the festivities, so I said goodnight to her and left her alone to visit with her kitties and went downstairs to make sure everything was set for the night.

Upon hearing the sound of the great front door lock being thrown, an unexpected feeling of sadness washed over me. For the first time in a very long time, the house *felt* empty. There had been so much hustle and bustle over the past summer; first the raid, then the cleanup, and then the filming. Evenings of Edie running from room to room, planning her costumes, preparing songs to be performed for the camera (many of which never went before the camera)—her general high energy about being filmed—it was all over now and that felt strange. There was a finality and a sadness that I hadn't anticipated. I sat alone for a long time at the dining room table and listened to the silence. When you're swept up in all the excitement, you don't stop to ask how long it will last. Now it was over, and somewhere deep inside I knew that an important chapter in all our lives had come to an end. How lovely, I thought, that the filmmaking ended with a celebration of Mrs. Beale.

The Maysles did return a few more times that year, but usually just to visit and inquire about the Beales' welfare. Once, during a cold November afternoon, they filmed Edie outside the mansion as she discussed the harassment she often felt from neighbors. She was particularly upset about the neighborhood children who would often throw things at the mansion and, Edie believed, tortured and killed a few of her cats. But that great celebration of Mrs. Beale's seventy-eighth birthday was the last time I saw the Maysles in the house filming. The "principal photography" had been completed, and the Maysles returned to New York City. As Mrs. Beale put it at the time, "The circus has left town."

With Edie during filming. (Maysles estate)

From the film *Grey Gardens* (1975). (Maysles estate)

Edie, pre-"raid,"
in the kitchen at Grey Gardens.

Gould's piano in the library at Grey Gardens,
after the clean up.

The lion in winter.

One of my favorite photos of my "sister" Edie,
my "mother" Edith, and myself. (Maysles estate)

Cleaning up the kitchen after "the Raid."
(Note: "Perfection," the behomoth stove, had already begun
a slow descent through the floor into the cellar below.)

In Rome, during my eighteen-month stint abroad.
(Collection of the author)

scarves and hoods (which leads one to wonder whether she shaves her head), she emerges as a self-made nun in heat."
Film Comment

"Edie twirls a baton, sings the VMI marching song and swims in the sea with a stroke that Fitzgerald's Daisy Buchanan must have used."
Newsweek

"A shot of her in the ocean, swimming with a perfectly schooled crawl stroke, suggests in one beautiful, quiet sequence that not all of the promise of her background and youth has vanished."
Film Comment

Mrs. Beale: *"But you never fell for a man. France fell but Edie didn't fall."*

Edie: *"This is my mother, just a girl from a good French family. It's a very beautiful face."*

Best wishes to my good friend "Jerry" – Wishing you also the best of luck –
March - 16th 1976 – Edith Bouvier Beale – East Hampton

A cherished momento - a note from my beloved "Mother,"
Edith Bouvier Beale, shortly before she died.
(Collection of the author)

With the one and only Madame.
I was one of the few people with
whom Wayland would entrust
with his creation.
(Collection of the author)

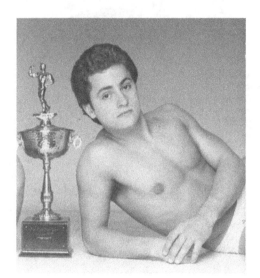

Winning
"Mr. Club Baths" in 1977.
I got this trophy,
and free room and board
for one year!
(Collection of the author)

On Confetti, my beloved Arabian horse, in Riyadh.
(Collection of the author)

With my partner, and best friend, Ted O'Ryan Sheppard,
at the Maysles Institute (2010).
(Collection of the author)

My years driving a cab. This led to my reunion with Albert Maysles and
the beginning of a whole new/old chapter of my life.
(Collection of the author)

CHAPTER FIVE: LEAVING THE GARDEN

To my seventeen-year-old mind, I felt that things at Grey Gardens could never return to the way it was before the Maysles's arrival. First of all, the house was different. The massive cleanup was followed so quickly by the pandemonium of the filming that there really wasn't time to reflect on the huge changes that had occurred as a result of clearing out the house. Rooms that once felt cramped and claustrophobic due to the cascading piles of debris, now felt almost cavern-like in their dark emptiness. All of the damaged draperies that had cloaked the windows in the library and dining room were replaced by slabs of plywood that allowed no light inside, so the downstairs resembled a cave. With no objects to absorb the sound, every word or utterance echoed through the house, which added to the isolated and lonely feeling. Before the cleanup, the exterior of the house appeared to be a part of nature, with the ropes of vines wrapping in and out of the structure, sometimes through the walls and the holes in the roof opening to the sky. But now, with much of the overgrowth of wisteria and bittersweet cut down and cleared away, Grey Gardens looked naked and exposed. In an attempt to encourage some new growth, I nailed a clothesline rope from one of the peaks of the roof and hung it so that vines growing would cling to it, but it was really to no avail. For better or for worse, things were different.

I was also concerned about the Beales. I felt very confident that Mrs. Beale would go on just as before the whole adventure began, but Edie worried me. After weeks of attention focused solely on her, the sudden withdrawal of it would have had to feel jarring—kind of what I imagined someone going "cold turkey" from an addiction must feel. For this reason, I kept mostly to myself after the Maysles left, and went back to tending chores around the house just as I had done before. Still, there was a noticeable change in the atmosphere at Grey Gardens. I detected a distinct coolness developing in the relationship between the Beales. Edie still attended to her mother's basic needs as before, and Mrs. Beale still called out to her when help was needed, but the animated discussions and debates, so much a part of their relationship, were noticeably fewer. I wasn't sure what caused this apparent cooling off. I know that Mrs. Beale did not approve of much of Edie's behavior during the days of filming; the scanty costumes, the flirting with David and Albert, the provocative performances of songs—perhaps this led to the distance between them. I didn't know and I didn't feel it was my place to pry. Plus, I had other things on my mind that summer, and one of them was named Terry Wallace.

A few months before, Charlotte had introduced me to a young man from Maine who had come down to East Hampton looking for summer work. Charlotte knew Terry and his family, and she encouraged him to come to East Hampton in the hopes that he could find work at the Geddes estate. From the moment I first set eyes on this strapping young man, with shoulder-length blond hair and sky-blue eyes, I felt an instant attraction. After a time, it became apparent that he was interested in me as well. We began spending most every free moment we had in each other's company and my attraction grew stronger and stronger. He would often accompany me to Grey Gardens in the afternoon. If I had a particularly difficult task to accomplish, he would pitch in and help me out. He first accompanied me to the mansion just after the cleanup, so the house was not in as extreme a state that it was in when I first met the Beales. Still, the living conditions of the Beales must have been alarming to him, although he never let on. Terry was extremely camera-shy and managed to stay out of camera shot when the Maysles were filming that summer, although he frequently helped them out with equipment. Edie seemed to like him, but she would never allow him in the house. (Later, I discovered that she suspected that Terry and I were removing books and other items out of the mansion through the library window—an accusation that was not only untrue but fairly ridiculous.)

It was, I suppose, inevitable that Terry and I would eventually give into our raging teenage hormones, but at the time I had no idea how to make the first move. I was, after all, raised in a strict Italian Catholic household, and despite—or maybe because of—my earlier sexual experiences with my neighbor, every erotic thought that crossed my mind was mixed with deep guilt, fear, and shame. But also, like a good Italian Catholic, I knew how easily feelings of guilt, fear, and shame could be overcome with just the right amount of "liquid courage"—and there was certainly plenty of that around.

As a sedate vacation resort, the area around East Hampton had its share of night spots, even a few places that could be classified as "gay clubs," or bars where at least one or two men were on the lookout for a quick hook up. Two such places were the Hampton Attic and the Out of This World Inn, just a stone's throw away from each other in nearby Wainscott. Terry and I would borrow Charlotte's car and hit the Hampton Attic for a long night of dancing and drinking gin gimlets (despite my under-age status, I was very familiar with the drink as I made them frequently for Mrs. Beale.) Once we were sufficiently sloshed, we would wind our way on foot to Out of This World, which was much more somber and dark, and we'd dance more and drink more. This was a rustic, single-level shack that had trees growing right through the bare wooden floor, hence "Out of This World."

Behind the main building and under a canopy of thick trees, there was a series of abandoned cabins strung together barracks-style. One night, after a particularly long session dancing and drinking, we made our way to the abandoned shacks. It was very dark and I was drunkenly leading the way past the row of cabins when I turned around quickly and found myself literally nose to nose with Terry. We stood there for a moment, but it was all we needed. I had never felt those emotions before, nor had I ever expressed my feelings to another human being. The liquor had allowed the emotional walls to drop, and any fear and hesitation evaporated into the cool night air. It was all so powerful and overwhelming. And wonderful.

Terry was able to find summer employment as a maintenance and repair man at a motel on Montauk Highway called the Cozy Cabins. This job provided him with a room in which to live for the rest of the summer with the promise of seasonal employment if he so desired. I had my hands full that autumn at the Geddes Estate and especially at Grey Gardens; there was much work to do in order to ready the house for the onslaught of the Northeast winds that would arrive in a matter of weeks.

Winter was a challenging time in East Hampton. Not only was the weather brutal, but being a summer destination, the place resembled a ghost town. The streets were empty, and most of the shops were closed for the season. In an attempt to buoy our spirits, when Christmastime arrived I cut down a large evergreen tree and set it up in the bedroom across from Mrs. Beale's bed. I decorated it with strung popcorn and paper plates and an occasional knickknack or trinket that I found lying about in an attempt to bring some holiday joy into the mansion, but it had very little effect. As had occurred the year before, a kindly stranger dropped off a fully cooked Christmas dinner for us, and we enjoyed it gathered around the space heater in the center bedroom. Unlike the previous year, however, our holiday celebration seemed hollow, with none of the warmth and cheer of before. Edie was moody and irritable, while Mrs. Beale seemed vague and distracted, and our festivities ended long before the winter sun set. That long, cold winter of 1974 was just not a happy time at Grey Gardens.

For me, the refuge of a warm and cozy home was not to be experienced. I had warmth and comfort at the Geddes house, but I was virtually alone there during the winter months. At Grey Gardens, I had Mrs. Beale and Edie for company, but the harsh living circumstances in that old house had gone from invigorating to exhausting; I was just plain tired of battling the elements. And, to be honest, after being in such close quarters with the Beales for so long, I was finding myself growing a bit restless and bored. At eighteen, I was craving an excitement and exhilaration that East Hampton just could not provide. Terry was back with his family in Maine, and although I knew that he would return in the summer, that felt like a lifetime away and I was lonely. The intense physical and emotional connection that I had felt with him only seemed to whet my appetite for more: I wanted escapades and explorations and experiences like the ones I now fantasized about on a near constant basis. Luckily for me, adventure was waiting for me just a short two-hour train ride away in Manhattan.

I can't remember the very first time I screwed up my courage and ventured into Manhattan on my own, but after hearing Edie enthuse about the pleasures of New York City, and meeting the Maysles and hearing about their exciting adventures filming around the world, I knew it was only a matter of time before I took the plunge. Their stories stirred something inside me that grew more and more insistent, until finally I had to give in to it and see for myself. It's not like I had never experienced a little nightlife, but an East Hampton bar was pretty tame compared to the things that I knew were going on in the big, bad city.

After finishing up my duties at the Geddes house, I would hop on my bike and head to the East Hampton train station, where I would take the Montauk line of the Long Island Railroad into Penn Station. At first, I rambled around the West Village, the heart of gay New York in the 1970s, and sometimes end up in a bar or a dance club. It was in one of these bars that I found out about the Club Baths, which became my home base in New York City for the next few years.

The Club Baths was located an old reconverted townhouse near Houston Street and First Avenue, and it was the first fully gay-owned and operated bathhouse in New York. I knew no one in Manhattan and I could hardly have afforded a hotel room, so going to the baths was inexpensive way to stay in the city. And for a young man just discovering his sexuality, it was also very exciting. Today it is hard to describe the experience of a bathhouse in those years, and most people get the wrong idea. The Club Baths (and others like it, such as the Continental, where Bette Midler performed early in her career) was much more than a bath house. It was a social club for men. It was our "clubhouse" and I made many friends the years that I went there. You entered up a short flight of stairs, paid your membership fee at the front counter, left your wallet and valuables there, and were escorted by a clerk to your locker or room and handed a towel. There were carpets, piped-in music, and soft lighting. If you took a locker, you undressed, put the towel around your waist, strapped the key to your ankle using the elastic band it was attached to, and headed to the ground floor to the showers. There were two steam rooms behind the showers, hot and hotter, as well as a hot tub nearby. Everything downstairs was clean, well lit, and covered in white tiles. It was not the dank and dirty den of debauchery that many people imagine. In fact, the Club Baths was quite a plush environment, as nice as many hotels in the city but at a fraction of the cost.

The rooms, which were actually windowless cubicles separated by a metal partitions, were upstairs on one of two additional floors. Each cubicle had a door that locked, a light with a dimmer switch, a very simple, single bed with sheet and pillow but no blanket. You could stay there for eight hours, but if you fell asleep and overstayed the allotted time, an attendant would come and knock on your door. There was also an outdoor garden area and a cafeteria that was open twenty-four hours. It was all very civilized. But of course, on the other side of that civility there was sex. Everywhere.

The Club Baths hosted various contests, and that first year I entered the "Mr. Club Baths" beauty contest. But I was too shy and introverted and didn't even place. The following year, I was feeling a bit surer of myself—a bit cockier with experience—and I entered the contest again, only this time I won! The night of the contest there were many handsome young participants, and though I was a young pup, I was by no means muscular or what I considered beautiful (even though Mrs. Beale would often tell me I was). No, what won it for me was personality. That night I made sure that I shook hands, smiled, and talked with everyone that I could. And that evening I won the contest. I was the new "Mr. Club Baths." It was more than just a title; there was also a cash prize and a free room in the bathhouse for one year. I had a place to come and stay for free in Manhattan for a whole year! But even more than that, I found that winning the contest opened doors for me that I could never have imagined.

One gentleman I met there found me a job as an artist's model at the New School for Social Research, a progressive university near Greenwich Village. In no time, I had a following of students who requested me as their model. One of the instructors at the school offered me a position modeling privately for him at his studio on LaGuardia Place. He was a mentor of sorts for me in the arts, and he awoke a fascination and a love within me for sculpture that I carry to this very day. Plus, he provided me with a steady salary, and that, combined with my work at the New School, gave me a very reliable income. Ever since I was sixteen years old, I was basically on my own, carefully walking a tightrope of subsistence. There never seemed to be enough money, and on those occasions when there was it never lasted very long. Now I was not only making good money, but I had virtually no living expenses due to my free year of lodging at the Club Baths. For the first time in my life I felt flush with money, which was intoxicating. And in the 1970s, there was no better place for a young, single man with a little extra money to be than New York City.

Of course, I didn't spend all of my time at the Club Baths. I also explored the city. I remembered Mrs. Beale telling me about her family's altar in St. Patrick's Cathedral. She had been married in the nave of St. Patrick's and it had been many years since she had been there, but she spoke with great reverence and admiration for the church. I promised her that I would visit the church one day and look for her family altar. She asked that when I did to please bring flowers to the altar on her behalf.

I'll never forget arriving at the massive cathedral and being bowled over by its enormous size. Roughly six-stories tall, it was the biggest room I had ever been in, and I tried to picture a young Mrs. Beale, who now spent the majority of her days in one small room filled with cats and clutter, walking down the grand cathedral aisle on her wedding day. It was unbelievable that she'd been married here. I made my way around the cathedral, overwhelmed by the artistry and beauty of it all, and after some searching, I finally discovered the Bouvier family altar. I was fascinated. It was small, but so beautiful, with an intricate wrought-iron gate covering the ornate marble altar-front. Although alone, I said out loud to Mrs. Beale, "I am at the altar. I do not have any flowers, but I will kneel here and pray for you and our lives." Throughout the years, especially in times of stress, I have returned to this very special place to pray and, remembering Mrs. Beale's request, I leave even the smallest flower at the altar in tribute. That first time, however, I felt overwhelmed at the spectacle and emotion of the experience. I was eager to tell her of the rush of love that I felt simply standing in the presence of such astounding beauty.

When I finally got back to East Hampton and shared the experience, she seemed pleased—if preoccupied. Edie told me that for some time her mother had not been feeling well, but Mrs. Beale refused even a suggestion of medical attention. It was just old age, she assured Edie— Mrs. Beale was approaching her seventy-ninth birthday after all. She said that she had survived on her own all these years without assistance from anyone (not entirely true, but that wasn't the point) and she wasn't about to start now. Despite her frequent attempts to override her mother's authority, Edie always deferred to Mrs. Beale's wishes in serious matters. She was "the Mother" as Mrs. Beale often said of herself; she was boss, and they both knew it.

Mrs. Beale's ill health made me wonder once again about the lack of support they received from any other members of the family—particularly Edie's brothers Phelan and Bouvier Beale. Edie told me that Bouvier lived somewhere in Oklahoma and hadn't been back to Grey Gardens in at least twenty years, whereas Phelan was just a short distance away in New York City. Why did he never come to East Hampton to check on his ailing mother and sister? True, I had not seen my own mother in over two years, but that was due to my father. Did things have to become dire, such as a raid from the Board of Health, for the Beale brothers to get involved with their own mother's welfare?

I left the mansion that day after visiting with Mrs. Beale in a private fury about everything—the raid, the massive cleanup, Lee, Jackie, even the Maysles. After *all* this, I thought, things were practically the same as they had always been. But I was wrong. Things were actually much worse.

Now Mrs. Beale's health appeared to be in decline. She had always had difficulty moving about and kept herself confined to the upstairs rooms of the mansion for as long as I had known her, but she had great vitality and *joie de vivre* regardless. She may have been physically limited, but her spirit was always robust. Suddenly, it had become a real struggle for her to leave her bed, so she spent weeks at a time in her bedroom. Moreover, whereas she was always maintained a full-bodied, zaftig figure (she frequently expressed her disdain for women who did not), she was clearly losing weight due to a loss in appetite. I became concerned and the thought of losing her hit me. I admit that I sometimes grew restless during my visits when Mrs. Beale recited verse or scripture, but I was a kid from the streets of Brooklyn. Who knew poetry? The songs Mrs. Beale would sing were wonderful because of the passion with which she sang them, but again, they weren't the types of songs that a teenager would be familiar with.

At about this time, however, I became very conscious of the precious moments that we spent together. Time seemed to be speeding up; one day I was horsing around with Terry on Georgica Beach, invigorated by the heat of the sun as it beat down upon our sweaty bodies, and the next, it seemed, I was watching my breath escape as I struggled to move the space heater from one spot to another in an attempt to find a working electric outlet. One morning I was waking up in my room at Geddes, my head throbbing from the effects of an all-night party at the Hampton Attic, the next I was frantically searching for my underwear and jeans on the floor of my room at the Club Bath, scrambling to make my 9:15 train at Penn Station. At times, it felt like I was on the old Scrambler ride at Coney Island; everything was moving lightning-fast around me, hurling me from one place to another to another—just stopping short of hitting the wall in front of me. Frightening. Exhausting. Exhilarating.

Although filming of the movie had technically been completed the previous summer, David and Albert Maysles made occasional trips back to the house to shoot a follow up scene or two and to take photographs of Edie for publicity of the film. Edie loved the latter in particular. She said it reminded her of her late teenage years when she was a fashion model for charity events in New York City and East Hampton. One very cold November day, the Maysles filmed Edie gathering debris and garbage from the front yard, and they also took some photos of her in her tattered fur coat. They decided that one of the photos that Albert took from this visit would be used as the poster art for the movie. It was a portrait of Edie standing in front of the house looking sullen, and it became an almost iconic image over the years as *Grey Gardens* became a cult phenomenon. Truthfully, this picture made me sad because it didn't include Mrs. Beale, who was as much a part of the film as Edie. But they picked this image, and that seemed to "seal the deal" of Edie as the "star" of the film.

The Maysles periodically phoned to keep us updated about the progress of the film over the following year. It seemed to me to be taking a long time to finish the film, but then again, I knew nothing about film. Then in late 1974, David called to wish us all a "Merry Christmas" and announced that the film was going to debut at the New York Film Festival the following summer. The Maysles wanted Edie and Mrs. Beale to attend the premiere, though it must have been obvious to them that Mrs. Beale never left the house and certainly was in no condition to attend a movie premiere. Before that event, however, they wanted to show us a "rough cut" of the film. Edie was beside herself with excitement, while Mrs. Beale was more reserved about the news and gave little enthusiasm for the idea. A date was set and the film, now officially called *Grey Gardens*, had its world premiere in the upstairs hallway at Grey Gardens the following April. Unfortunately, I was not in attendance that day, but from what I later heard (primarily from Edie), the screening was a great success. In fact, Edie's exact words were, "The Maysles have created a masterpiece!" Mrs. Beale said very little to me about the film other than that she was happy that her singing was included, but I sensed that she was less than pleased over how Edie's erratic behavior came across on the screen.

Before leaving the house that day, the Maysles invited Mrs. Beale and Edie to the official New York premiere at Lincoln Center that September. Due to Mrs. Beale's declining state, it was decided that Edie would attend the premiere alone and Mrs. Beale would remain in East Hampton. There was no question about who would care for her while Edie was away—taking care of Mrs. Beale was not only something that I was used to doing, it was my pleasure ... and truthfully, I looked forward to the chance to spending time alone with her without Edie around, which never happened.

Even though the gala was months away, Edie began running about the house excitedly, discussing what she would do in New York and planning the costumes she would wear. Among the clothing that Mrs. Onassis had given her over the years was a beautiful red dress that Edie loved, and she informed us that she was going to wear it to the premiere. But first she had to get back into shape, she repeated over and over. Mrs. Beale began referring to Edie as "Celebrity." Over the next few weeks, Edie drove both of us crazy with her preparations for her trip to New York.

One day, she told me with utmost sincerity that her trip there was a permanent one, and she would never again set foot in her mother's house. Then without explanation the next day, she adamantly declared she wasn't leaving and didn't care about the film, the Maysles, or New York City. Mrs. Beale and I, of course, knew this wasn't the case. Despite her nerves about the premiere, I thought it highly unlikely that Edie would pass up the opportunity to play the movie star. And with Mrs. Beale far away in East Hampton, this was truly Edie's moment alone in the spotlight. It would be *all* hers. To stand out on her own and be adored—it was what she had sought her entire life.

And it was finally happening.

The summer seemed to fly by in a blur and before we knew it, the date of the premiere had come. Even though the Maysles had invited Edie to the premiere, they did not arrange transportation for her to get to New York City. Consequently, there was a great flurry of phone calls between David and Edie. After much drama on her part, the Maysles said that they would provide a hotel room and transportation to and from the event, but that it was Edie's responsibility to get herself to New York City. It didn't matter, Edie said with a wave of her hand, she *would* be chauffeured from her hotel room to the premiere in a car—and *that* arrival was what everyone would see. She decided that she would make her grand return to New York, *her* city—to the premiere of *her* film—on a Hampton Jitney bus.

Despite my difficulties with her, it was this determined attitude of Edie's that made me love her most and forgive her almost anything. No matter what curveballs life threw at her—and there were many—she always turned the situation around and moved on. How else could someone justify living all those years as she did—in utter and humiliating poverty and degradation—unless they found the positive side to the situation? It was that power of positive thinking, you could say, that turned a flea-infested house into a palace, an old cotton bath mat into a turban, an ill-fitting skirt into a grand cape, and a torn shower curtain into the wrap of the Queen of Sheba. She didn't take lemons and make lemonade—she made Champagne! I will always—always—have nothing but love and admiration for the combination of determination and delusion with which she did it.

Though she was travelling to New York by bus, she contacted a car service (complete with chauffeur) to drive her from Grey Gardens into East Hampton to meet that bus. Wearing a pair of expensive brown elephant boots (another gift from Jackie), a tan trench-coat, a red kerchief tied around her neck, and a golfing cap, Edie gave me a hasty goodbye and climbed into the black town car. As I watched it drive away, the thought that perhaps she would carry through on her claim of not coming back to East Hampton flashed in my mind. It was hard to imagine I'd just seen the last of her. Then again, only a few hours earlier she declared that she had changed her mind and wasn't setting foot in New York City. Now "Celebrity" was actually on her way.

With Edie gone, there were a few things I was determined to accomplish before her return. Other than doing my best to give the downstairs a good cleaning (relatively speaking), I was finally able to defrost decades of accumulated ice from the refrigerator—a task Edie resisted no matter how many times I offered to do it. I fed the cats and the raccoons as Edie had instructed me. My major objective, however, was to spend as much uninterrupted quality time with Mrs. Beale as I could. I surprised her by rummaging through the attic and locating many of her old recordings, which delighted her. She told me long stories about "this movement" or "that passage" in the music, as well as discussing Mozart and Tchaikovsky. As it was late summer, we managed once or twice to make it into the sunroom—her favorite spot— and sing a few songs together, enjoying the last warm days of the season.

After my encounter with Mrs. Onassis as well as my trip to St. Patrick's Cathedral, I was very curious about the Bouviers, and I asked her about her family history. She told me wonderful stories about her mother, whom she loved very much and who encouraged her desire to sing. She was less forthcoming about her father, but she never spoke negatively about him or her brother "Black Jack" Bouvier (nicknamed so because of his ever-present suntan), who had been the cause of many of their financial hardships. She told me about the afternoon recitals she would give in the solarium at Grey Gardens, and the dozens of people who would come and listen to her sing. At the end of the day as the evening chill would set in, I would plug in the electric heater and position it between the two twin beds until the room got warm and comfortable. Mrs. Beale and I would talk—she on her bed, me on Edie's—until she would begin to get sleepy, at which point I would unplug the heater and quietly creep down to my old army cot positioned under the canvas tent in the library. It was in these times, when we were singing together or talking quietly at night in the glow of the space heater, that she was in the best of spirits. I tried hard to keep things as upbeat and lively for her as possible. On the whole we had a marvelous few days together.

Edie eventually had to returned to Grey Gardens after living the high life in New York. When her car arrived at the house, she sat inside it for more than a few moments; I am not sure if she was talking to the driver or if she just didn't want to get out. She finally did get out of the car and made her way to the front porch, where I was waiting for her. I had imagined that she was probably feeling very sad coming back home, but there was something more. I am not sure what transpired in New York, but she returned in an anxious state.

The first thing she asked me was whether Albert

Maysles had phoned. This seemed odd. Hadn't she just left him and his brother in the city? I told her that he hadn't called and asked her how things had gone. I was excited to hear the stories of her trip and was dying to hear what people thought of the film, but she dismissed my inquiries. She seemed more distracted than usual, staring off into space. After a time, Edie told me that she was treated very well in New York. The screening, she said, was a "marvelous success." People raved to her about the film for hours at the reception afterward, and that she was certain is was going to be "a landmark in cinema." (I confess, I laughed at the thought; little did I know how right she was!) Then, her mood darkened and she said in a very low voice that she was worried about money. I thought this was a strange transition of thinking. "Edie," I said, "we've never had enough money. Why on earth are you worried about it now?"

Apparently, sometime during the trip, someone put the idea in her head that she and her mother should have received additional compensation from the Maysles for the film, and as of yet, none was forthcoming. She asked me if I would call the Maysles and ask them when to expect payment for the film, a request I quickly declined. I didn't have the authority to contact the Maysles with such a question, and I told her so. "We should be getting five thousand dollars," Edie blurted out at me, "and I want to know when we are getting it!" I had not been privy to the financial agreement that she and the Maysles had made regarding the film and was certainly not the person to be investigating it (I received two hundred fifty dollars from the Maysles for my appearance in the film, incidentally). I had no idea how—or who—had put this idea into her head, but she looked at me with an intensity that frightened me a bit. And then, as suddenly as the anger flared, it dissipated. "Well," she said with a sigh of resignation, "anyway, the house looks good. How's Mother?" Before I could answer, she was up the stairs and out of sight.

After Edie's return from New York, my visits with Mrs. Beale grew less and less frequent. I had neglected my chores at the Geddes house, and with autumn quickly approaching, I had much to do. Terry and I had resumed our relationship when he returned to East Hampton that summer, and that situation, as well as my "extra-curricular" activities in Manhattan often took precedence over spending time with Mrs. Beale. For some unknown reason, Edie seemed more contrary with me than ever after returning from New York. When I did find the time to visit, she would leave me waiting on the front porch before granting entrance. Above and beyond all of this, there was another, much more disruptive event that happened at this time that made me even more hesitant to spend time at Grey Gardens: Lois Wright moved in.

I could count on one hand the number of times I had spoken to Lois, so I knew little about her. I was aware that the house that she shared with a friend had recently burned down and not long after she asked Mrs. Beale if she could move in temporarily until she found a new home. Although I had nothing against Lois personally, I never really felt comfortable in the house after she moved in. She and Edie made a formidable team when they wanted to, and they often served as a barrier in to my attempts to spend time with Mrs. Beale. Lois made her home in the bedroom known as the "eye" of the house as it overlooked the front lawn, so she could see who was coming and going. She also set up a studio in the kitchen, where she could do her painting (she had recently decided that she was an artist). It felt to me as if she was taking over and her presence in the house made me more and more uncomfortable.

In truth, it wasn't as much fun at Grey Gardens as it had been a few years before. Mrs. Beale rarely left her bedroom, Edie's moods were more mercurial than ever, and Lois' presence seemed to exacerbate them. In the past, Edie's mood swings were frustrating, but now they seemed downright baffling to me. Whereas she was once outspoken and unfiltered in her comments, she now was rude and downright mean to me for no reason. For the first time, I began to sincerely wonder about the state of her mind. While I had always found her behaviors odd and eccentric, the thought of a real mental illness had never seriously crossed my mind before. After spending those few days alone with Mrs. Beale, however, and hearing more about her past, I started to wonder. And worry.

In the meantime, Brooks, who had been so helpful with the cleanup and stayed around afterward to help me out with the yard chores, was also spending more time working around the house. Brooks was a very nice man, but he drank a lot and would often show up at the house a little worse for the wear, his breath revealing his intoxicated state. In the past, this situation caused alarm with Edie (Mrs. Beale, with typical discretion, would simply smile and say, "Too many cough drops today, Brooks?"). Now I would come to the house and find him sleeping on the stairway landing. When I mentioned this to Edie or Lois, they would brush it off as if it were nothing unusual. Lois had a history of alcoholism, but was proudly sober and I believe that she encouraged Edie and Mrs. Beale to give Brooks additional responsibilities after she moved into the house. Thus, Brooks went from sometime gardener to errand boy to virtual caretaker for Edie and Mrs. Beale.

To be fair, Brooks was often a great help around the house and a kind and decent man. It was Brooks who suggested getting a wheelchair for Mrs. Beale in order to give her some degree of mobility and self-sufficiency, and it was a great idea. The chair had a high back and small wheels on the side, resembling more of a "rolling chair," and we all decided to refer to it as that. We knew that Mrs. Beale would be much more open to the idea of using it if it weren't thought of as a wheelchair, even though that is essentially what it was. Sure enough, she quickly took to the chair and was soon in much better spirits as she acquired a mobility that she hadn't enjoyed in some time, although she still restricted herself to the second floor.

I was grateful that Mrs. Beale had more people to

help her. Plus with so many people around, there was the unexpected bonus that I was no longer the primary target of Edie's paranoia. Still, it was difficult not to be hurt by the sudden changes at the house. If food was needed, Lois would go to Newtown Grocers to pick it up. If something needed fixing, Edie would call on Brooks to fix it. I began to feel like a fifth wheel and thought that perhaps it was time for me to think about moving on.

That winter, the film *Grey Gardens* opened at the Paris Theatre on East 58th Street in New York City. Once again, Edie attended the premiere, but unlike the last time, I was not asked nor did I volunteer to care for Mrs. Beale. Lois was to be caretaker while Edie was gone. It felt odd, certainly, but if Mrs. Beale was being cared for, that was all that mattered. I had begun modeling for the classes at the New School and was very much enjoying my new "career" and the attention I was receiving, particularly from the handsome male students. I was also getting attention of a different, unexpected nature.

Since its release, *Grey Gardens* had stirred up a bit of controversy in its no-holds-barred depiction of our life; many critics called the film shocking and exploitive. There were articles and reviews of the film in *The New York Times*, *The Chicago Sun Times*, as well as a few notable national magazines such as *People* and *Harper's Bazaar*. It is only now that I am aware of the notoriety that developed around the film, particularly in cultural circles. I was a nineteen-year old kid from Brooklyn, so knew nothing of film culture. At the time, I was so wrapped up in my own burgeoning life (and what nineteen-year old isn't?) I was fairly oblivious to the controversy about the film unless it was brought directly to my door. It was when my family began making comments to me about the movie that I started to wonder.

About this time, my brother Robert was getting married and I had the first face to face contact with my family in many years. My father was his usual belligerent and quarrelsome self, as much as my mother was caring and gentle. I realized upon seeing her how much I missed her, but knew that there was no way I could be close to her without having to deal with my father. At my brother's wedding, I did my best to ignore my father and his ignorant comments about the Beales and my life in East Hampton, but it was my other relatives who I couldn't ignore. People at the wedding cornered me, asking all sorts of questions about Mrs. Beale and Edie and my relationship with them, as well as wanting to know all about the Kennedys, the Bouviers, and so forth. My mother told me how proud she was of the man I had become and how much she missed me. She also kept telling people that I was staying with "the Beatles" and I had to correct her constantly that they were "the Beales," not "the Beatles." It all became very uncomfortable. After all, it was my brother's and new sister-in-law's day, and I didn't want to upstage them. Besides which, I hadn't even seen the movie yet, so I was confused about many of the questions they asked me and the things they said.

I really hadn't considered that my participation in

the film would come to anything, since in my mind it was always Mrs. Beale and Edie's film. I think because I had lived it, the film held little curiosity for me at first. But as time passed, people began to recognize me as "the Marble Faun" and said so. I paid little attention to anything that strangers said to me, but eventually I began to wonder just what some of their comments meant and just how this character of "the Marble Faun" came across. I knew that eventually I would have to see the movie.

I finally saw *Grey Gardens* at the Village Cinema in East Hampton later that spring. It may seem hard to believe, or maybe not considering the negative light placed on the town by Edie, but there was very little commemoration of the film being shown there. I only found out about it after stumbling upon an ad in the local paper advertising its screening times. So, when I finished work one afternoon I went into the village, paid my dollar fifty, got some popcorn, and entered the nearly empty theatre to watch *Grey Gardens* at my local movie theatre just like everybody else.

It is really difficult for me to put into words how I felt watching so much of my life—so much that I held near and dear to my heart—displayed for all to see. Up until then, it had been my secret, private little world—a safe space cut off from everything and everyone else. Now, suddenly, it was all out in the open. Edie was—well Edie. In the film, she is exactly as I expect her to be, though the intimacy of the camera magnifies her behaviors. She is definitely mesmerizing; for better or worse, her absolutely unique and idiosyncratic character makes it difficult to take your eyes off her. However, out of all of us, I felt that Mrs. Beale comes across the best. Even in those scenes that were, to me, of questionable taste, her inherent elegance and grace shines through. For example, the scene in which Mrs. Beale, in a fit of anger at Edie's behavior, allows her bathing suit to fall to the floor. Thankfully, the Maysles turned their cameras away before the scene became too explicit, and Mrs. Beale maintained her composure despite the kerfuffle. Still, it was upsetting to see Edie so clearly baiting her mother and behaving in such an obnoxious manner.

There was also the scene in which Edie declares, "To *hell* with the Marble Faun!" with such vehemence that I was stunned. What in the world had I done to incite such condemnation? I had no idea of the depth of Edie's suspicion and antipathy toward me until that moment. Her cross attitude about the things I did (such as the washing machine), the things I didn't do (such as steal books from her room) was a total surprise to me. Until then, I thought that I was helping the Beales—and indeed I had! But for the thousands—perhaps millions—of people who were seeing this film, the effect was exactly the opposite. There I was, huge on the screen, looking for the most part incredibly uncomfortable and like some sort of teenage opportunist. Edie had told me that "the Marble Faun" was her name of love and endearment for me; now it felt like a colossal joke.

Throughout the screening, there had been a few

scatterings of laughter here and there, but for the most part, the film was greeted with silence. When the film ended, I sat for a bit, slouched down in my seat and let the other five or six attendees leave before I stood up. I left the movie theatre stunned and numb.

A light rain was falling during the long walk back to Grey Gardens, and I attempted to get hold of my feelings and gather my thoughts. Had I not told Mrs. Beale that I would be returning to the mansion that night, I would have gone straight to my room at the Geddes estate. I didn't want her to worry about me, however, so I slowly made my way back toward West End Road.

When I finally arrived, I stood in front of the house for a few minutes. I remembered the first time I had stood in the very same spot, that summer night when I first looked up to see the eaves of the roof pointing up through the thick overgrowth and wondered what was inside this strange and extraordinary place. Back then, it was just "our" house—now it belonged to everyone who saw the film, and in a way, so did our lives. I returned to Mrs. Beale's home many times after that night, but in the most fundamental ways, things had changed forever for me and Grey Gardens.

By some miracle, Edie had left the back door open for me and I tried to be as quiet as I could as I entered the kitchen and made my way to bid Mrs. Beale goodnight. I didn't know what I was going to say to her once I got upstairs; I felt angry, but more than anything, I felt hurt. Betrayed. I imagined that Mrs. Beale was hurt too on my behalf. In fact, for a moment I imagined that this may have been what helped widen the gulf between her and Edie after the movie came out. To my surprise, Edie was waiting for me on the landing. I had told her before I left that I was off to see the film—was she expecting a confrontation? We looked at each other, and after a bit she asked me if it was raining outside because I was soaked. I hadn't even noticed. I said yes, it was raining, and she quickly went to the dining room and brought back some paper towels. I took them from her and began to wipe my face and neck. She stood right in front of me, watching me intently, waiting, I think, for me to ask her: Why had she said all those things about me? Did she really feel that low about me after everything I had done—everything we had *been through* together? The raid? The clean up? The endless hours I spent in the summertime cleaning up the yard and trying to make the place somewhat livable? The lengths I went to on those frigid winter days to make sure that she and her mother had some sort of warmth and comfort to get them through the night while I nearly froze in the library? The evenings we all sat together and talked and laughed and sang for hours like a family? The scenes all played through my head like a movie—a different movie—one that was a true and accurate portrait of what our life was *really* like in Grey Gardens. As I looked at her, I desperately wanted to ask, "Why, Edie? Why?" But I couldn't. I was too hurt and confused to even begin. Instead, I took a deep breath, handed her back the paper towels, and said, "I'm going to tell Mother goodnight, if it's OK with you." Edie nodded and I turned and went upstairs.

A few days later, I was sweeping the floor of the downstairs vestibule when Edie came whirling by me. She was in the midst of putting "costumes" together for her latest project, a nightclub act in which she would sing and dance and tell stories about her life. Although no offer had been made—or even hinted at by *anyone*—she was adamant that an offer would be coming in a few days. The success of the film, she argued, would guarantee it. As she stood next to me, pondering the costume choices for her cabaret debut, I decided to finally broach the subject of the film.

"You know, Edie, I saw the movie a few nights ago ..." Edie stopped and looked at me but remained silent. I asked, "Have I offended you in some way? That scene on the upstairs porch: 'To hell with the Marble Faun,' you said. Why did you say that? Are you uncomfortable with me here? Do you want me to leave? Because in the movie it sure seems like you do."

Maybe she was caught off-guard by my directness because she remained uncharacteristically silent, waiting for me to continue. And then I asked the question that had been eating away at me for days.

"Edie ... don't you like me?"

She continued to stand there in silence, perhaps trying to formulate a response. Then, after what seemed like an eternity, she took a deep breath and said, "Do you like this dress? I think I want to wear it for my club act. What do you think?"

Now it was my turn to stand there speechless. I just couldn't fathom what she had just said—or hadn't said. I knew that Edie was capable of anything, but I wasn't prepared for this. And before I had the chance to say anything, she turned from me and started upstairs.

"I'll go ask Mother what she thinks," she said. "She'll know."

I stood there for a few moments, stunned by her reaction, and then I laughed to myself. It was no surprise at all, really. I would probably never get an answer from her and probably never know why she said the things she said or if she even believed her own remarks. What did I expect, after all? That was Edie.

One of the unfortunate outcomes of *Grey Gardens* was that it re-focused the attention of the villagers on the Beales and their extreme living situation. After the cleanup, things had become relatively peaceful around the neighborhood. With the Beales now back in the spotlight, the traffic on Lily Pond Lane had definitely increased as people drove slowly by to take a look at the mansion; a few of them even got out of their cars and took pictures on the lawn. To Edie, who lived for so long feeling that the world had left her behind, these types of incidents were exciting. What wasn't exciting, however, were the people who came right up to the door or attempted to crawl in a window to get inside. Additionally, the trespassers and vandals returned. To my knowledge, there was never any direct contact between these intruders and either one of the Beales, thank goodness, but it definitely raised Edie's anxiety level. I was glad that when I was gone, she had Lois and occasionally Brooks around. Not that Lois was much help; she seemed to be indifferent to any of the difficulties we faced each day until they directly affected her.

She had taken over the pantry as her "art studio," and because the kitchen was a major thoroughfare for Brooks and me to travel when we were working, it was quite annoying to have to climb around her several times a day. She was completely unsympathetic to the situation, and frankly I was getting more and more irritated. I was about to blow my top until one day the situation took care of itself.

One day in late autumn, Lois was working away in her studio and Edie had was in the process of drawing a bath for herself upstairs. The problem with this was that the hot water heater had ceased working, and the only way to get warm water into the upstairs bathtub (the only working bathtub in the house) was to heat pails of water on the kitchen stovetop and carry them up to the bathroom. This, of course, was my job. I heated three pails on the kitchen stove and (climbing around Lois at her easel) carried them up the back stairs into the bathroom, which was located directly above the pantry. I poured the hot water into the tub just as Edie entered the bathroom and gave me a look that indicated I was to leave as she was going to bathe. I quickly headed out of the bathroom and went downstairs to the library.

Suddenly, Lois cried out, "My paintings! They're being ruined. The water is ruining them!" She ran into the downstairs vestibule and screamed upstairs, "Edie! The water!"

Apparently, there had been a flood of water through the kitchen ceiling from the bathroom above. Lois was soaked and so were her paintings. Edie appeared at the bannister in a towel, screaming at Lois to be quiet because her mother was resting. Lois screamed back that her paintings were ruined. It was quite a scene; I had never seen Lois angry. My offer of help was met by her with a swift and vehement "No!"

I ran upstairs and into the bathroom. Edie must have turned on the faucet in the tub to cool the heated water a bit and then left the room. The upstairs tub was small and prone to overflowing, especially when Edie stopped up the drain with newspapers. I shut off the running faucet, then made my way into the bedroom to check on Mrs. Beale, who, despite the commotion, was fast asleep. I wasn't sure if this was good or not; I was glad she was resting, but the fact that she could sleep so soundly through such a racket disturbed me. I tucked the blankets around her tightly and put my hand on her shoulder. "Goodnight, Mother. I love you," I said and gave her a kiss on her forehead. As I made my way downstairs and out the door, I could still hear Lois shrieking about her paintings, with Edie telling her, "Calm down, Lois, it's only water!"

Not long after, the cold-water pipes in the basement burst, which stopped all the running water in the house— including that which ran to the toilet. Brooks was able to fix the problem a few days later, but emotions in the house were beyond frayed and close to a boiling point. Fortunately, a stabilizing force entered the Beales' lives at this time, and her presence proved to be somewhat of a godsend. Her name was Doris Francisco, and she was a friend of Lois.

Doris was a large, imposing woman—very grand and formal, and also quite intimidating. She reminded me of the actress Colleen Dewhurst. She had been acquainted with the Beales for many years, but it wasn't until she saw the film *Grey Gardens* that she felt compelled to come to the house and attempt to help out. She was particularly concerned over Mrs. Beale, and Doris's calm but forceful nature was a welcome dynamic to the turbulent times. In many ways, Doris became an attending nurse for Mrs. Beale—often cooking nourishing meals for her, something that Mrs. Beale needed very badly. The days of ice cream and *pâté* for dinner were over, and Doris brought much needed common sense to her diet. She also fed the cats, kittens, and raccoons, as well as driving into the village for supplies and cleaning up after Edie. It was quite amazing to see this regal and patrician woman dumping bags of Wonder Bread on the floor while calling out to the raccoons that it was dinnertime. If she was repelled by this or anything else she encountered at Grey Gardens, it never showed. She did it all with grace and aplomb. Moreover, she refused compensation of any kind, stating that she did it only for her concern for Mrs. Beale. It was almost as if, in His divine wisdom, God had decided to bring this angel to Mrs. Beale to comfort her in the final

THE MARBLE FAUN OF GREY GARDENS

days of her life. That is most certainly what Doris felt like to me.

By now, I was spending more time in Manhattan than in East Hampton. With the Geddes house closed up for the winter, and Brooks, Lois, and now Doris on hand to care for Edie and Mrs. Beale, there was really no reason for me to spend as much time at Grey Gardens. In New York, I had steady modeling work, free room and board at the Club Baths, and a very active social life to keep me busy. I had recently met a very attractive young man named Robert one afternoon in Central Park and was spending a lot of time with him in his apartment. But it was more than the lure of the city that kept me away. I let my hurt feelings regarding Edie and *Grey Gardens* get the better of me, and that kept me from visiting East Hampton as much as I should have. I knew Mrs. Beale wasn't in the best of health, and I telephoned the house often to check on her. I soon discovered the Mrs. Beale was having some memory confusion—she was not sure what time it was or what day it was. While this disturbed me, at the same time it didn't alarm me too much, as there were no clocks at the house and even those of us who weren't dealing with the effects of ageing had difficulty knowing what time it was. Still, I decided to check on her in person.

I arrived at the house to find it remarkably cold—even by the cool Long Island autumn standards. What's more, Grey Gardens was in a state that I hadn't seen since before the raid: a filthy mess, garbage piled in the corners and in complete disarray. Edie had let me in and said that her mother was not getting any better. She was afraid that she was going to lose her very soon. Only at Doris's insistence that a doctor be brought out did Mrs. Beale agree to receive medical care. He determined that Mrs. Beale had pneumonia and stomach ulcers, for which she was given antibiotics, but she still flat out refused to go the hospital.

Leading me upstairs, Edie stopped and in a very low voice said that she had, on the advice of the doctor, contacted a lawyer and had her mother draw up a will. As she told me this, she began to cry. I felt at a loss as to what to do. I wanted to comfort Edie—hug her—but something inside me prevented me from reaching out. I had never seen her cry; I had seen her upset and frustrated to the point of anger, but I had never seen her break down in tears. She seemed like a little girl as she stood there in front of me, and I now wish that I had reached out to her that day, but I didn't. After a few moments, Edie regained her composure and led me to her mother's bedroom.

Contrary to the rest of the house, the bedroom was heated to an uncomfortable degree. There were more kittens in the room than I'd ever seen, jumping around from bed to bed. Doris was sitting beside Mrs. Beale applying lotions and salves to what looked like huge welts on the side of Mrs. Beale's body. Later I was told they were bedsores acquired from weeks in bed without being able to move. It was disturbing to see to say the least, but not as disturbing as seeing Mrs. Beale's deteriorated condition. She was almost unrecognizable, her body nearly half the size of the woman I had seen only a few months before. She was so pale and drawn, I nearly couldn't speak, but she motioned for me to come over to her.

"Little Jerry," she said softly. "Hello, little Jerry."

Despite the grim atmosphere, I laughed. How many times had she greeted me with those words? I had not heard them in a while, and it was so nice to greeted with them once again.

I said hello to Doris, who acknowledged me gruffly, and Mrs. Beale and I talked for a bit as I knelt by the bedside. She asked me how I was doing, where I was staying, how my family was. I didn't go too deeply into the specifics of my personal life, because I didn't feel comfortable discussing such details, but just assured her that I was doing fine, working in the city and staying in a nice apartment with "some friends." This seemed to comfort her.

I didn't stay very long. It was incredibly uncomfortable in the room, and not just due to the heat. I felt as if Doris was scrutinizing me the whole time. I wondered if perhaps Edie had poisoned her opinion of me; at this point I didn't put anything past Edie. I justified my short visit by telling myself that I would come back very soon. Though we didn't talk for long, Mrs. Beale said something that stuck with me for the rest of my life. We had never discussed the film much before; in fact, after the initial screening in the hallway, I don't recall her ever mentioning it again. Mrs. Beale was someone who appreciated the past but didn't dwell on it. She was much more interested in what was happening in the present. But at this visit, she seemed almost eager to discuss it. As we were reminiscing about the movie and everything that had happened since the Maysles first arrived, she stopped and looked at me for a long moment. "In your lifetime," she said, "the film and our relationship will be of interest to many people, Jerry. Someday, it will be yours to watch over and take care of." I absently nodded at her remark—more concerned with making my exit than really grasping what she was telling me. Today, I get chills thnking about how accurate her prediction was.

Despite my best intentions at the time, I didn't return to Grey Gardens for many weeks. Soon after New Year's 1977, I called Edie to see how things were going and the tenor of her voice truly frightened me. She sounded scared and lost; the fear and anxiety that I heard in her voice that day reminded me of horrible day of the Suffolk County Health Department's raid. I knew that I needed to get out to East Hampton as soon as possible. I tried to calm my own fears by assuring myself that all would be OK, that this was just another visit, but deep down I knew that wasn't true. Instinctively, I felt I was going to Grey Gardens to say goodbye.

The weather was unseasonably mild a few days later when I arrived at the house to find Edie alone with her mother. As we climbed the stairs to the second floor, she told me that she was about to take her mother out to the sunroom in the rolling chair. She said it would be nice for the three of us to spend some time in Mrs. Beale's favorite room. When we reached the landing, I found Mrs. Beale sitting in the rolling chair, a blanket wrapped around her body. Her head was covered by the blanket like a hood and I knelt beside her and gently put my hand on her knee. I was startled by how thin her leg was. During an earlier visit, when I had lifted her into the rolling chair, I was shocked at how easily I had picked her up and carried her into the chair. She seemed so delicate then, but now her fragility was scary. I tried not to show my distress, however, as I gently patted her leg. She opened her eyes and looked at me, but I sensed no real recognition in her face. Then suddenly, I saw it; the unmistakable light in her eyes and a smile forming at the corners of her mouth. I smiled back and said softly, "Hello, Mother."

Edie and I wheeled her down the hallway into the sunroom and into her favorite corner near the window. It was a clear, cloudless day and the sun heated the room to a point where it felt like a mid-spring afternoon, not the winter day that it actually was. Edie talked nonstop about nothing of great importance, just noise to fill the silence. I barely paid attention; it was all I could do to keep it together in front of Mrs. Beale. She was too weak to do much else but look at me and smile, yet that was all that she needed to do. Those same eyes that had looked into mine on that first visit almost five years before with such compassion and tenderness, they were the same eyes that looked at me now. They conveyed the same tenderness to me as the first day we met, but this time there was something more. An acknowledgement, perhaps, that this was the last time we would see each other? I don't know—but the look in her eyes at that moment is something that I have never forgotten. I wanted to say something to let her know I was aware that this was goodbye, but all I could do was smile back at her. It occurred to me as I was kneeling beside her that this was the exact spot where I had first met her as she sat in the corner of the sunroom listening to her radio and enjoying the feeling of the sun on her legs.

Edie suggested that since it was such a mild day, we go onto to the porch so that her mother could enjoy the sunlight and some fresh air. Though she was too weak to speak, Mrs. Beale gave a slight nod that indicated that she would like that. I wheeled her with great care, worried that I would cause her pain. As we made our way onto the porch, I noticed the "sea of leaves" had completely vanished for the season and there was Edie's "unseen chair" starkly exposed. How odd, I thought, the cycle of nature. In just a few short months, the barren branches below us would be overrun with green and white, once again hiding the chair from sight. Life—then death—then life again; nature always got a reprieve. As I looked over at Mrs. Beale, how I wished it were true for humans as well.

After more small talk with Edie, I felt the overwhelming desire to leave. I told myself I should stay a bit longer, but I just couldn't do it. I could feel my emotions welling up inside me, and I was too close to a complete breakdown. This was something I just wasn't prepared for. Something in me demanded that I remain strong: "Be a man," I could hear my father's voice in my head. "Men don't cry!" And I didn't. I remained calm and asked Edie if she would like me to help get her mother back inside, but Edie said she wanted to stay outside a bit longer. I looked at Mrs. Beale to find her smiling at me once more. I reached up and gave her a gentle kiss on the cheek—as I had so many times before—and said, "Goodbye, Mother. I'll see you soon." Although she was too weak to speak, I know that inside she said goodbye as well.

By late January, Mrs. Beale's condition was becoming dire. A doctor had been summoned to the house to re-examine her. Taking one look at Mrs. Beale, he advised Edie that her mother needed to go to the hospital immediately. He was afraid that the bedsores had become so bad that septicemia, or blood poisoning, would set in if it hadn't already. Mrs. Beale needed medical attention in a matter of hours, not days. No matter, Mrs. Beale refused. The doctor left, and, in a panic, Edie contacted Doris, who in turn phoned a priest at the Most Holy Trinity Catholic Church, Father Huntington, in hopes that he could assist. From what I later heard, Father Huntington and a parish nun arrived at Grey Gardens on February 2. After a short visit with Mrs. Beale, he convinced her to go to the hospital, which she did, by ambulance later that day.

On the morning of February 5, I awoke at Robert's apartment in Manhattan with a strong inner urge to telephone Edie and find out what was going on. After many failed attempts to reach someone at the house, I finally got an answer. It was Lois, who informed me that

Mrs. Beale had passed away earlier that morning. There had been a bad snowstorm on Long Island, and the doctor had phoned to tell Edie that Mrs. Beale could die at any moment and that she should get to Southampton Hospital as soon as possible. Lois and Doris risked the hazardous roads to get to the house, so that Doris could drive Edie to the hospital. Lois stayed behind and a few hours later, Edie telephoned to tell her that Mrs. Beale had passed away.

When I heard the news, my mouth went dry and I was at a total loss. I was so young, and death was something of which I had no concept. I had never lost anyone I had loved, and I didn't have the emotional tools to express my feelings and the overwhelming sense of loss that engulfed me. My friend who had shown me so much kindness and generosity, to whom I felt a bond so strong, was only a memory now. How was that possible? Of course, I knew that she had been in decline, but I just couldn't digest the reality of her death. Over the next few days I didn't know what to do other than to swear that I would honor her memory for the rest of my life.

Mrs. Beale's funeral was a private observance that was held at the Most Holy Trinity Church in East Hampton on February 8, 1977, one of the coldest days I can remember. Edie's brothers, Phelan and Bouvier, who had arrived shortly after their mother's passing, had determined that the ceremony would be private due to the fact that Jacqueline Kennedy Onassis was to attend the service and her presence, along with the recent publicity from the film, was sure to attract the paparazzi. It was also decided that it was to be a closed casket ceremony. Mrs. Beale received a long obituary in both *The New York Times* and the *The New York Daily News,* and sure enough, outside the church on the day of the service there were television cameras and newspaper photographers and reporters, all vying to get a shot of Mrs. Onassis, or Lee Radziwill, or Edie. I borrowed an ill-fitting dark brown suit from my brother and made the trip out to East Hampton.

As I pulled up to the church in an old hatchback that I had recently acquired (I had finally graduated from my bicycle to an automobile), I saw Lois and Doris, along with some gentlemen who I determined later were Edie's brothers, as well as two women whom I later discovered were Mrs. Beale's sisters, Michelle and Maude. A bit closer to the chapel, standing apart and a bit in shadow, I recognized Mrs. Onassis and her sister Lee, as well as two other familiar figures: Albert and David Maysles. Edie was nowhere to be seen, and feeling a bit self-conscious in my borrowed suit, I slipped past and inside the church, where I found her talking to Brooks. Edie was highly agitated about something, and I felt it was best not to intrude on their conversation. I found out later that she was distressed by the presence of the Maysles. Apparently, they had arrived at the house earlier that morning, and she had refused to let them inside. In fact, for reasons that were known only to Edie, she had barred them from the funeral entirely.

The choice of music for the ceremony had been decided long beforehand. Some years prior, Mrs. Beale,

Edie, and I were listening to some of Mrs. Beale's old recordings when we came to her favorite, "We Belong Together." She declared that she wanted this recording to be played at her funeral and assigned me the task of making sure that it happened. Of course, I agreed to her request but didn't think much of it after that until I was inside the church. Looking over to the vestibule, I saw the familiar old record player from Grey Gardens sitting there. Suddenly, I remembered my dear friend's request. What should I do? I felt so out of place—so isolated from the rest of the mourners. Was I the interloper again? No one had even acknowledged my presence when I arrived. Should I be so bold as to carry out her request and play the record during the ceremony? I wondered, would Edie even remember that her mother had made this request of me, or would she cause a scene and have me removed from the church? For a moment, I thought of walking out of the church, getting back into my car, and heading back to New York. Who would notice if I just left?

As I was thinking this over, I slowly made my way to the vestibule and looked down at the record player. Sure enough, there on the turntable was Mrs. Beale's record. I felt a hand on my shoulder and turned around to see Edie standing behind me. I froze for a moment, uncertain as to what was going to happen next. She then leaned toward me and whispered in my ear, "Mother loves you a great deal."

I suddenly felt flushed. It was the kindest thing she had ever said to me. I had always known that beneath all

Edie's dramatics and histrionics was a very real, much wounded person. Living all those years in the darkened corridors of the great house, caring for her mother, she had sacrificed more than anyone would ever know. But in that brief moment of connection at the record player, I think I experienced my first real understanding of her. We had been through so much together that even in our most contentious moments I had felt a kinship with her. What was so wonderful was that, at this moment, she was acknowledging that kinship as well.

I nodded to the record player as means of asking permission. She nodded back her approval, smiled, and walked away. Once again, it was the three of us in a private unity. We were a family again ... one last time.

When the ceremony began, I sat in the rear of the church, off to the side as to have quick access to the record player. When the time came, I made my way over to it and softly lifted the stylus off its perch and onto the moving record. Mrs. Beale's voice rose to the rafters of the church:

> We belong together,
> we're happy together,
> and life is a song,
> when we are together,
> we know we are where we belong ...

Hearing Mrs. Beale's voice echo throughout the church brought her back to me. Sitting beside her in her bedroom as she sang along with her records, recited her favorite poems and passages of verse, or just conversed with Edie and me. For a moment, she was alive again and filling a room with her presence as so many times before. I told myself to hold onto the feeling; I wanted to save it forever.

After the song was over, I returned to my seat. As I did, I looked at Mrs. Onassis sitting in the pew directly in front of me. When I made my way past her, our eyes met for the briefest moment and she gave me a smile of acknowledgement. It was then that I noticed the tears in her eyes.

After the service, we made our way to the cemetery behind the church. Much like Mrs. Beale, her final resting place had so much inherent elegance. Towering over us as we walked to her graveside were great beech trees, their long, thin branches naked and looking as if they were scratching the surface of the grey sky. I imagined how they would look in the glorious days of summer, Mrs. Beale's favorite time of year. Their branches would spread out like enormous crowns of green, shading the bright sunlight but allowing little flicks of it to burst forth as the wind made their leaves dance. It would be beautiful.

That day, however, it was so cold that great chunks of frozen earth were piled up near the opening to Mrs. Beale's resting place. Next to it, on the tombstones nearby, I saw names I that I had heard many times before: her brother John Vernou Bouvier III, her mother Maude Sergeant Bouvier, and her father, John Bouvier, Jr. As we stood around the gravesite, the priest arrived and begun delivering a sermon. He took out his aspergillum to sprinkle the holy water over the grave, and I began to feel a surge of emotion well up inside me. I had not been able to cry for Mrs. Beale since I was told of her passing; from childhood, I had built up such a wall against pain of any kind that my emotions were not easily expressed. Suddenly, I began to sob—unable to stop or stifle it. I could feel many of the mourners looking at me, and I was so embarrassed, but I could do nothing about it, so I just let go.

After a time, the pain subsided a bit and I could get ahold of myself. As the priest concluded the ceremony, we began to disassemble. Feeling very self-conscious about my outburst of emotion, I quickly started for my car. Before I could get there, however, Edie stopped me and put her hand on my shoulder. I appreciated her attempt to comfort me, but I felt so embarrassed that I dismissed any offers of comfort and assured her that I was fine. Edie invited me back to the house to have something to eat, but I declined her invitation. It would feel so odd and painful to be in the house without Mother being there, and I told her so. Also, I didn't cherish the idea of spending time with her brothers, particularly Phelan, who was as rude and condescending to me at the funeral as he had been on the telephone. I thanked her but said that I had to get back to the city. I wanted to ask her what her plans were now that her mother was gone. It was hard to imagine Edie alone at Grey Gardens. She was resourceful, for sure, so I knew that she'd get by somehow. I couldn't fathom, however, how she wouldn't be haunted by her mother's absence. They had their disagreements, but they thought alike, spoke alike, and lived in the same fantasyland— isolated from the rest of the world. The entire time I had known her, Edie had been yearning to be free of Grey Gardens and to forge a life of her own. But I wondered, was she ready or even capable of starting that life? After our years together at Grey Gardens, I couldn't picture her anyplace else.

We walked a bit further in silence and as we approached my car, I turned to her. "What do you think you will do now?" I asked.

"I'm going back home," she said quickly, as if it were the silliest question she had ever been asked. I was about to say, "I mean, after today," but I stopped myself. She knew what I meant, I realized. She smiled and walked away. She would be just fine, I thought.

As I got in my car, I looked back one more time to see her standing in the church driveway, about to get into the car that would take her back home. She was wearing a long, tan raincoat, buckled at her waist and a simple black hat with a pin at the side. I took a mental photograph of her that day so I would never forget this extraordinarily complex creature whose kindness and generosity toward a scruffy, dirty-faced kid forever changed the course of his life. Much as I knew that my final visit with Mrs. Beale would be my last, I felt deep inside me that this would be the last time that I would ever see Edie.

Or so I thought.

Many years later—in the mid-1990s—I was back in New York City working as a cab driver. By this time, I was a well-seasoned cabbie and made my way around the streets of Manhattan like the best of the daredevil drivers. I had a fare in my cab and we were travelling crosstown on East 60th Street, approaching Fifth Avenue. It was raining very hard that evening—one of those drenching New York torrents that feels as if it's soaking you from head to toe even though you're inside a cab—and its constant downpour made traffic more perilous than usual. I had my window partially open to allow some cool air to flow in and alleviate the humidity inside the cab.

As I reached Fifth Avenue, the traffic light changed to red. Sitting at the foot of the intersection, my eyes wandered over to the entrance of the Pierre Hotel, located just across the street. There was a grand canopy at the entrance of the hotel that stretched from the doorway to the curb. As I sat in my cab waiting for the light to change, I was struck by the sight of someone standing beneath it. This person was dressed entirely in bright red—red shoes, red stockings, red skirt, red blouse, and a red coat draped over her shoulders. The woman was certainly striking, dressed entirely in red, but it wasn't her outfit that startled me: it was her head. She was completely bald. Moreover, wrapped around her bald head was what appeared to be a golden cobra headband that coiled around her skull, culminating near the top of her forehead in a tiny little snake head with bright ruby eyes.

The passenger in the back seat of the cab must have been as dumbfounded as I was by the sight, because after a few seconds she asked, "*Who* is that … *What* is that?!"

I knew who it was. Almost twenty years had passed since I had last seen her, and she certainly looked a bit more worn down and aged from the passage of time, but *who* she was was unmistakable to me. Even in New York City, a place full of oddballs and eccentrics, she stood out as the truly rare character she was—and always would be.

"Edie," I smiled and said to myself. "It's Edie."

The moment I uttered those word, she turned her head and looked straight at me, as if she had somehow heard me say her name. Our eyes locked, and for a brief moment we seemed to experience a silent communication and recognition of each other. But before I had the opportunity to call out to her through my open window, she turned and got into a cab that had stopped at the curb. My light had turned green by this time, so I stepped on the accelerator and began moving through the intersection. As I did, I briefly glanced over at the taxi now departing the curb and headed into the night.

"Goodbye, Edie," I said quietly. "Goodbye."

Edith Bouvier Beale died on January 14, 2002 in Bal Harbor, Florida. She was once again living near the sea, where she could take daily walks on the beach and enjoy one of her favorite pastimes, swimming against the strong current of the Atlantic Ocean. She was eighty-four years old.

CHAPTER SIX: LIFE OUTSIDE OF THE GARDEN

The death of Mrs. Beale severed my last real tie to my life in East Hampton. In actuality, I had ceased to feel a part of East Hampton for quite a while. Mr. Geddes sold his house in 1976, which meant I no longer had a job on his estate, my relationship with Terry had run its course, and I was—in effect—living with Robert in Manhattan. There wasn't a precise moment when I made the decision that part of my life in the Hamptons was over; as with so much in life, it just happened. If you had told me at the time that Grey Gardens would come to define not only the child I was but also the man I was to become, I would have dismissed the idea. Sure, it was a pivotal part of my youth, but when I drove away from Mrs. Beale's funeral that day, I was twenty-one years old and had my entire life before me. Furthermore, by 1977, the film *Grey Gardens* had pretty much disappeared from sight. In the days before home video, movies played at the theatre, and when they were done, they were gone from view until they showed up on television at some later date. But those were mainstream films with wide appeal; I don't ever remember seeing documentary films such as *Grey Gardens* shown on television. What kept *Grey Gardens* even remotely alive in those years before home video was gay men.

Ironically, as a gay man myself, I didn't appreciate the affection that other gay men had for the Beales, Edie in particular. I knew she was outrageous, of course, but after years of living with her, I had become inured to her eccentric ways. This was not the case for other gay men seeing her for the first time. In 1978, Edie created and performed a cabaret act it in a small gay nightclub in the West Village called "Reno Sweeney" (just as she had told me she would all those years before). I was not living in New York at the time and did not see the show, but I was told by those who did that it consisted of some stories, a few songs, and some fitful dancing. They also remarked that, while it was not what you would call a smash hit, it was enthusiastically received by its audience made up almost entirely of gay men. As for me, I came to find out about the *Grey Gardens* gay cult following when I mentioned that I was "the Marble Faun" once or twice during an otherwise standard date. Well, that did it. Forget sex, suddenly the encounter turned into an interrogation session about the Beales and Grey Gardens. After the fourth or fifth time this happened, I decided to keep my identity secret until *after* I had my orgasm. It was easier that way. Still, in these years Grey Gardens was a part of my life in only the most peripheral way; I was young and ready to tackle what life had to offer. And in the late 1970s in New York City, that was a lot.

Though I was still occasionally modeling for art students, it was hardly steady work and certainly not enough for me to bankroll a life in Manhattan. A few years earlier I had made the acquaintance of Trudy Heller, owner of the club in Wainscott, the Out of the World Inn, where Terry and I had spent so many wonderful, hazy, drunken nights. She liked me and encouraged me at the time to make a plan for my future. She knew of my hard work at Grey Gardens, and liked my professional attitude, she told me. With my boyishly-scruffy appearance, she said I could easily make a lot of money working as a bartender at one of her clubs. In addition to her East Hampton club, she also owned an eponymous night club in Greenwich Village and had connections at another club just around the corner from it called the Bon Soir, where Barbra Streisand famously launched her career in 1961. Trudy assured me that I could work as a bar-back while I trained as a bartender during the day. It now seemed to me to the perfect path, so I soon tracked her down at her club and told her I would take her up on her offer. I enrolled in bartending school during the day, worked as a bar-back at night, and slept ... well, frankly wherever I happened to end up after last call. Sometimes I went back to Robert's, sometimes I went to the baths, and sometimes I went home with a guy that I had met that night at work.

Many acts passed through the clubs over the years, one

of the most memorable being the female impersonator
Lynn Carter. Lynn was an extraordinary performer—the
first female impersonator I had ever seen. In fact, he was
the first female impersonator to play Carnegie Hall when
he opened his show there in 1971. I was fascinated by the
fact that when he was off stage, he was a very masculine
individual. I was working as a bar-back at the Bon Soir
when Lynn first arrived, and I was introduced to him.
I could tell immediately that there was an attraction
between us, but not wanting to jeopardize my job, I didn't
respond to his overtures toward me. But eventually I gave
in, and he and I began and on again/off again personal
as well as professional relationship that lasted for almost
two years. Lynn was booked at a wonderful hotel in
Provincetown, Massachusetts, called the Pilgrim House,
and to my surprise, one day he asked me if I was interested
in spending the summer working for him there. It wasn't
a difficult decision, and the next thing I knew I was
running lights not only for Lynn's show but also other
shows that were booked into the theatre that summer,
including the wonderful Julie Wilson and an enigmatic
but hugely talented ventriloquist named Wayland Flowers
and his sidekick, a raunchy little puppet named Madame.

Wayland Flowers and Madame had not yet achieved
celebrity, and when I heard of their booking I thought
they were a magician act. I arrived later that day for a
dress rehearsal and noticed a handsome blond man lurking
about the stage—Wayland. He didn't say a word to me at
the time; he was strictly business. As made his entrance

onto the stage carrying his puppet, I hit the spotlight and focused it on him. He stopped dead in his tracks. "Not on *me*!" he bellowed. "On *Madame*!" I couldn't understand what he was saying. "What do you mean?" I yelled back. "Don't put the light on *me*! The light is on Madame!" He wanted the light on the puppet—always. During the rehearsals, Wayland was demanding, testy, irritable, and downright mean. Several times I felt my Italian blood boil, but I remained calm. I imagined that this guy and his ugly puppet would bomb in short order and would be on their way out in no time. I have rarely been so wrong in my life.

On the night of his opening, the Madeira Room was a madhouse. There were mobs of people standing, seating, crouching on the floor—waiting outside in lines to try to get into the hallway outside the theatre to just *hear* the show, let alone see it. I was shocked. Who was this guy? When it was announced "Ladies and gentlemen, Wayland Flowers and Madame!" I flipped on the spotlight and hit the puppet and the audience went wild. What followed was one of the most amazing—and hysterical—performances I have ever witnessed. Wayland had only "marked" his performance at the dress rehearsals, never once engaging the puppet as anything but a prop. Tonight, on that stage, that puppet was *the show*. It really was as if this tiny little person was sitting on Wayland's hand, complete with her own, fully developed, outrageous personality. It was truly astounding, and it was that night that I realized the difference between "good" and "great."

Having dealt with my fair share of eccentrics of the years, Wayland's odd behaviors didn't faze me much. For starters, he would relate to people almost entirely through Madame. If he was unhappy with something that happened during the show, I would get a real tongue lashing; but not from Wayland, from *Madame*! As Madame, Wayland could, and did, say the most shocking and raunchy things on stage and get away with it, but that was nothing compared with the vulgarity that came out of that puppet in private. I admit, it was difficult to keep a straight face while getting bawled out by a two-foot-tall hand puppet, but I did my best. And eventually, the kinks in the show smoothed themselves out, and my relationship with them both became cordial ... then friendly ... then something else entirely.

Provincetown was, and is, a gay mecca in the summertime, and among the hot spots was a bar called the Boat Slip, a fairly large space that also had a swimming pool. One afternoon I was swimming around the pool in my Speedo bathing suit, and I looked up to see Wayland and Madame at the bar, holding court with a small group of loud, and clearly inebriated, gay men. At one point, I got out of the pool to get a drink, and as I approached the bar, Madame's head snapped around in my direction. Well, Madame made a few cutting remarks about the size of my Speedo which led to an outright sexual proposition ... from a *puppet!* Of course, it really came from the man behind the puppet, and for one moment during our exchange when we briefly locked eyes, I saw the real man behind the facade.

And, that is how I ended up in what must have been the strangest ménage à trois in history: Wayland, Madame, and me. Now, I don't pretend to try to explain or justify why or how this all happened. The truth is, after many drinks at the bar that afternoon—all paid for by Wayland—I eventually found myself in Wayland's hotel room, naked on his bed, with Wayland on top of me and Madame … well … she was just about everywhere imaginable that night. It was surreal to say the least. To blame my willingness to go through with it all on the alcohol would be a cop-out; the truth was it was fun and funny and I enjoyed it. Wayland was not only a very attractive man, he was the biggest star in Provincetown that summer. People were always clamoring for his attention, and it was fun to be a part of that. From that night on, Wayland insisted that I always be included in whatever events or shows that they appeared in. Not only that, I was the only one he entrusted to hold Madame when he was not around. This was a great honor. Wayland viewed Madame not only as a prized possession, but as if she were a real person, and to entrust her in my care was a huge compliment. Alone in his room at night, Wayland would ask me to hold Madame while he slept; he was always afraid of crushing her and he felt she was safe in my hands. He would show me how to sit Madame on my arm, place my hands up into her head, and how to manipulate her arms and hands. It was a complicated process, but I soon got the hang of it. Often, as Wayland slept beside me, I would have private little conversations with Madame, attempting to duplicate her unmistakable "voice" as she answered back to me.

Also, it is not generally known, but there were actually *two* "Madames." There was the "Park Avenue" Madame, dressed in sequins and feather boas that appeared on television and in nightclubs, and then there was another "Adults Only" Madame, outfitted with a whip and in leather dominatrix attire. Wayland would employ this Madame at special clubs and parties to entertain much less family oriented audiences, and on a few occasions, she entertained me as well. It was a crazy summer!

At every performance, there would be celebrities in the audience, people I recognized such as Goldie Hawn and Lily Tomlin, and non-descript men in business suits that would come back stage and make Wayland offers to come work in Atlantic City, Las Vegas and even Hollywood for huge sums of money. It was clear that he was "on his way," and Wayland wanted me to come along with him. I would be lying if I said I didn't think about what it would be like to be a part of that whirlwind, but in the end I turned him down. I had a small taste of that sort of attention from my experience with *Grey Gardens*, and I knew that it wasn't the type of life for me.

And to be honest, the whole situation began to feel a bit sordid. I eventually found that I had to get drunk or high in order to have sex with Wayland ... and Madame ... and I could only imagine how much worse it may have become if I stayed with him. No, a summer fling was all it would be and that was fine because eventually summer would end. Sure enough, as soon as his run at "The Madeira Room" ended, Wayland and Madame flew off to Los Angeles to appear on the game show *Hollywood Squares*, and his career soared.

I never saw Wayland again, but of course I watched him on *Hollywood Squares*, and kept tabs on his success through his many appearances on television. In 1982, when he got his own television show, *Madame's Place*, I was overwhelmed with happiness for him; later, when I learned of his illness, overcome with concern. I thought about trying to get in touch with him, but by that time, 1988, I was in not in the best shape myself. It was with great sadness that I learned of his passing from AIDS in the fall of 1988. He was only forty-eight years old, and truly one of the most remarkable people I have ever met.

When the summer season ended, we headed for a ten-day engagement at Plays and Players in Philadelphia, where it became clear that something was going on with Lynn. He was irritable and short-tempered throughout the run. After the gig ended, we returned to New York for a brief rest, and after a few days, I got word that Lynn had suffered a heart attack and was in the hospital. Memories of Mrs. Beale's death came flooding back to me, and, though he eventually left the hospital, his great unharnessed energy was no more. He suffered a series of heart attacks in the early 1980s which further disabled him, and, in a cruel twist that was to become a through line in my life in the next decade, he died of complications due to AIDS in 1985.

I moved back in with Robert and resumed the carefree and untroubled existence that I had enjoyed before I left for Provincetown. Though Robert and I were living together, we were a "couple" in only the loosest sense of the word. The concept of a monogamous relationship with Robert never even crossed my mind; there was just too much sex to be had with too many different people. Between the bars and the baths and backrooms, New York City in the late 1970s was a sexual playground. There were also the abandoned piers on the Hudson River, the truck trailers that were parked nightly under the elevated Westside Highway, and, of course, one of my favorite places, the Ramble in Central Park, where I first met Robert. No, we were all having much too much fun enjoying the unprecedented sexual freedom of the era to concern ourselves with the boredom of monogamy. Of course, as we were to find out in the coming decade, freedom is never free. There is always a price to pay.

But that was a thought far, far away from my twenty-five-year-old consciousness. Life came at me fast and furious—I took everything that was thrown at me and more. Somewhere between East Hampton and New York City, I moved from idyllic country roads to the fast lane, and by the early 1980s I was moving at warp speed. Over the next decade, I found myself saying "yes" to every possible opportunity, chasing every possible dream and running faster and faster to catch up to ... what? I was running but what was I running toward? Or, was the reality that I wasn't running toward something, but running away from something else? And as long as I kept running, it could not catch me. So, for the next decade, I did. I ran from

New York to Maine, to Canada where I worked for the Canadian Pacific Railroad, back to Manhattan, then to Saudi Arabia, employed as a caretaker for the royal family, tending to the many priceless portraits, tapestries, and fine sculpture that populated the palace. That particular adventure refueled the passion I had for sculpture, first experienced all those years ago at the 1964 World's Fair. It also refueled my bank account, and after only thirteen months in Saudi Arabia, I returned to New York with nearly seventy thousand dollars saved, thanks to Robert's astute business sense.

While I was in Saudi Arabia, I had carefully sent the majority my earnings back to Robert in New York City for safe keeping. I trusted him unreservedly; I knew he would not only safeguard my money but perhaps make a few investments on my behalf that would make it grow. I was not mistaken; when I returned, I had quite a nest egg waiting for me. I couldn't believe it! I had never imagined that I would amass that sort of money in my lifetime. When Robert told me this, we whooped and hollered and acted like crazy people. How I wished that Mrs. Beale had been alive! I would have headed straight for Grey Gardens with my arms full of cash and showered her and Edie with it. But she was long gone, and the last that I heard of Edie was that she was living in Montreal finally learning to speak French (a skill that she could never master, to her great frustration). I had no idea what I was going to do with my Saudi Arabia windfall, but I didn't worry about it. Robert had hinted around about some ideas he had about how best to use it. I knew he was an astute businessman, so I was excited to hear them. But not right now. The future could wait for a few days; right now, I wanted to play. Back then, New York was still "Fun City"—I wanted to have some fun.

Within no time, I was back in my old nighttime haunts: the Club Baths, the Anvil, St. Mark's Bath, the Saint. Remarkably, nothing had changed. If anything, the clubs were even wilder than they had been only a few years before, but perhaps that was just because I had been starved for human contact for so long that everything—and everyone—looked appealing. At any rate, those first few weeks I was back in New York were a carnival of bacchanal delights the likes of which I had not experience before, and certainly never experienced after. To be honest, the experience—while exciting and fun— was also a bit frightening. It seemed to me as if everyone was partying harder and pushing the limits further for no other reason than the mere act of it. I sensed a note of desperation and it wasn't the joyous adventure it had been. Still, I didn't give it more than a passing thought. There was still too much fun to be had, and I was making up hard for lost time.

By the time I returned to Robert's apartment a few weeks later, I was totally spent, and ready to settle down and begin planning a serious future for myself. After all, I was no longer a teenage kid riding his bicycle around the neighborhood doing odd jobs to make money. I was getting older; in a few more years, I would turn thirty.

And with my windfall from Saudi, it seemed the perfect time to start a brand-new adventure—one that I hoped would secure my professional and financial future.

Robert's plan was a fairly simple one: we would go into business together. The business he had in mind was a furniture moving company, which seemed ideal. It would be a physical endeavor, something which I always enjoyed, and would also give me the opportunity to learn business management. Moreover, after a decade of economic depression, New York was experiencing an exciting new period of financial prosperity and growth. Seemingly overnight, neighborhoods such as Chelsea and the Upper West Side, which for decades had been gangland war zones, were becoming chic and much desired addresses. Parks such as Verdi Square, near 72nd and Broadway and nicknamed "Needle Park" for its profusion of drug dealers and addicts, was suddenly filled with baby strollers and young children at play. Most importantly for our new business, ramshackle tenements in these neighborhoods were being demolished to make way for dozens of brand new apartment buildings. New apartments meant furniture to be moved, and this is where Robert's brainstorm came into play. It was the perfect idea at the perfect time. Before I knew it, we had purchased a truck, placed ads in the local papers, and we began booking jobs. We had decided to call our business "AAA All Boro Trucking," so that in an alphabetical listing in the phone book or in the *Village Voice*, our company would appear first. This was another one of Robert's inspirations which quickly proved what a talented and savvy businessman my partner was; that was his domain. I focused on the day to day labor requirements and client relations that I had managed with a smile and accommodating demeanor. Who knew that my years of dealing with the erratic temperaments of Lynne Carter, Wayland Flowers, and a certain cousin of Jacqueline Kennedy Onassis would come to serve me so well in my own business? I laughed to myself when these screeching designers suddenly turned into purring pussycats the moment that I accommodated one of their ridiculous requests with a smile and a nod. So, you see, our success was equally accredited to both Robert and myself and our individual skills and talents.

As our business expanded and we began servicing high end clients on Park and Madison Avenues and all along the Upper East Side. One particular job in those early days stands out to me, as it was for Paloma Picasso, the daughter of Pablo. Needless to say, it was a surreal experience for me. Just to be inside her Park Avenue home and see the incredible artwork displayed on her walls—it was definitely a "pinch yourself" experience. Moreover, Paloma was a genuinely nice person, and because of her we began to book many jobs handling fine works of art— which was naturally a joy for me—and our little company really began to prosper. My financial investment quickly doubled, then tripled. It was a wonderful, exciting time. If I had only known it would be such a brief time as well.

Although most people probably would have thought of investing their money into the heady stock market of the time, or perhaps buy a piece of property for themselves, I didn't bother with such concerns. As hard as I worked, that was just as hard as I played, and after spending the day working my ass off lugging around 250-pound sculptures, I would spend the night working my ass off on the dancefloor or at a bathhouse. New York in the "last days of disco," as it has been called, was a kaleidoscope of decadence. From the perspective of thirty plus years later, it seems like a dream or like life on another planet, and in many ways, it was. The 1970s was a very depressing time for the city economically, but socially it really was "Party Central." When the economic boom of the 1980s hit, suddenly there was money to add even more fuel to the fire. From Studio 54 to the Saint—it really seemed like one long unending party, and I was at the perfect age to experience it all full tilt boogie! Robert and I were still operating at full steam; our business was really booming and I had plenty of money to spend on whatever hot and exciting new scene was in vogue. At the time, it all seemed like harmless fun. I was a member of the first generation of gay men who could be out and proud, and it was an intoxicating feeling.

What people do not often take into consideration when they criticize the sexual freedom of the 1970s and 1980s, is that it was a celebration of freedom after decades of repression. Only fifteen years before, to proclaim yourself an out and proud gay man could have landed you in jail, or worse, in a psychiatric ward at Bellevue Hospital. I experienced a taste of that as an adolescent; fearful that if my true nature was ever to be discovered I would suffer the same fate. Now, suddenly, after a few short years you could be free to be yourself without fear of recrimination … we felt alive. And what is a more basic and fundamental expression of being alive than sex?

So, it was a very different time. I soon decided to move out of Robert's small Gramercy Park Apartment to my own on the Lower East Side, without drama or incident. We were still very much partners in every sense of the word; committed to each other personally and professionally. New York was undergoing one of its periodic cultural revolutions, and the Lower East Side—for a long time an area of poor immigrants—was becoming a trendy place to live. It was still seedy, make no mistake about that— but it was a "hip" seediness, much like the Upper West Side had been in the late 1970s. Now that the yuppies had taken over that area, the displaced artists and musicians were moving to the Lower East Side. Unfortunately, so were the drug dealers, and our new neighborhood near Tompkins Square Park was particularly rife with them. But that didn't bother me; what people did to make a buck and get by in life was no business of mine; I had a great new apartment—lots of money coming in—and a very active and exciting social life. What was there to be bothered about?

As it turns out, plenty. I had begun hearing whispers of healthy young gay men getting sick with unusual infections in San Francisco and Los Angeles in late 1981, but paid no attention to it at the time. Then, suddenly, stories of people contracting a strange new "gay cancer" began cropping up in New York City, too. At first, as people do when strange and scary new events start occurring out of the blue, rumors began to fly.

First, it was thought this cancer was caused from heavy use of the party drug amyl nitrate, also known as "poppers." Then, it was thought to infect only people who had sexual partners numbering in the hundreds or more. In both cases, I was a prime candidate. But for years, I remained healthy. Soon, all around me however, I began to find out that people were getting sick.

Within the second year of our business, Robert and I had obtained a second truck, which we paid for in cash, and drove right out of the showroom. We had hired young Puerto Rican boys to be our movers; they were young and energetic and grateful for the work. Our business was booming. Robert's skills and expertise in business, and my hard work had paid off handsomely. He was so bright; his organizational skills were impressive and in a matter of three years, he grew our business into a thriving enterprise. Moreover, I had begun to rely on him in all things—he was the backbone to my life.

Then, one spring morning in 1987, we found ourselves walking in midtown Manhattan. We had just surveyed a potential installation of fine art at a client's house and while we were discussing the project, Robert suddenly began speaking gibberish. At first, I thought he was joking around, but this was totally out of character for him, especially with a client. Afterward, we walked for many blocks in silence, until I began to discuss the project we had just left. Robert again couldn't speak in full sentences without jumbling words. He was always meticulous in his speech and manner; there was something very wrong.

Fearing that perhaps he was having a stroke, we decided immediately to head to the emergency room at Lennox Hill Hospital, which was thankfully only a few blocks away. Tests were done and it was determined that Robert wasn't having a stroke. We were relieved, but then the doctor gave us results from other tests that were performed. There were large lesions covering Robert's brain; he was diagnosed with a form of cancer called Kaposi Sarcoma. Robert had AIDS.

As time went on I began to notice more and more people dropping out of sight. Men that I had seen for years at the baths and the discos were suddenly nowhere to be found. And then you began to hear why: they weren't around because they were dead. Every day I ran into someone who would tell me of the death of another friend—and later when I would try to phone the person who had told me the news, they would be dead, too. Within a year, the entire gang that I hung out with was gone.

After a few weeks of hospitalization, I made the decision to take Robert home. I brought him to my apartment in the Village, and that first night he fell and was back in the hospital that night. He never left. To see someone you love, someone who was strong and healthy and in the prime of his life, slowly begin to resemble a sick and dying child is something that I would not wish on anyone. The week before Robert died he had asked me, "What are you going to do without me?" I immediately thought of Mrs. Beale, who would often say the same thing to Edie during one of their heated discussions. Edie would always respond with, "Oh, please, Mother. We all know you're not going anywhere." I found myself saying the same thing to Robert, and we laughed. But we both knew it was a lie.

After I somehow made it through his funeral, I raced home; I just couldn't face Robert's family at the memorial service. Within moments of getting into my neighborhood near Tompkins Square in the East Village, I located a drug dealer and purchased some cocaine from him. I took it home with me and telephoned some former tricks to come over and share it. The idea of being alone was just too much to bear. To a man, every one of the guys I called was dead. I didn't know what to do; the pain from loss was overwhelming. In desperation, I called an escort service and hired someone to spend the afternoon with me. As it turned out, I didn't leave the apartment for two weeks.

In the past, I had done drugs only occasionally. Almost everyone did—it was part of the "scene." I had never sought them out; you didn't have to because drugs were always around. Sometimes I would partake and sometimes I would not. I enjoyed my life and my experiences too much to want to dilute them with anything stronger than liquor. With alcohol, I experienced a hazy, fuzzy, slightly out-of-focus feeling that was enjoyable but not threatening. I still knew what was going on around me, but I felt removed—like I was hovering over it all, watching. Drugs had a much more profound effect on my senses, taking me completely out of reality and into my own private little world. I now wanted that total escape. I wanted to shut off everything. Voices in my head that told me that I was next to die from AIDS; the images of Robert in his final days—the funeral—the sobbing of his family. I had to stop it all from flooding my mind, and the only thing that could do that was drugs. A lot of them.

Drug addiction swept into my life and destroyed everything in its path. At times, guilt would overwhelm me and I would find myself on the floor crying out for Robert to forgive me and my destructive ways. In my more lucid moments, I would vow to stop my behavior and pull myself together before I lost everything, only to have my resolve crumble after a few hours. I was hooked; I was a drug addict.

I was destroying my life, with no one to care, and no one to care for me. I had completely shut myself off from my family, and my erratic behavior had scared away all the friends I had left who weren't dead or drug addicts themselves. When you're an addict, your drug becomes the only thing that matters in your life, and everything else falls to the wayside. Weeks passed into months and then into years; over the time I did indeed lose everything in my life. Finance companies repossessed our trucks and our equipment; the lease on our company headquarters was terminated and the leasing company took possession of everything inside. Most devastating, my entire earnings from my time in Saudi Arabia—including the windfall from the investments that Robert made on my behalf—was gone. In three years, I'd blown through all of it.

Over time, my addiction grew stronger. At first, it was just a mental battle. After a time, though, it became clear to me that I was becoming physically addicted and that scared me beyond belief. I had always been a strong and healthy young man; now I needed a "fix" before I could bring myself out of bed in the morning. I would lie there in true mental and physical anguish, tormented by the thought that I would never escape this hell that I created until I gave in to the temptation, and waited for the sense of calm and euphoria to sweep over me. Anyone addicted to drugs of any kind—be it alcohol, cocaine, heroin, or whatever—will tell you, however, that after a time, the "peace" you so desperately seek becomes more and more elusive and more difficult to sustain. So, you ingest more, or you mix it with another substance to get you where you need to go until that too starts to fail, so you take more … and more … until finally, everything stops working. Nothing relieves the horrendous mental and physical pain. That day is a desperate day; it is frequently the day that either ends in overdose or suicide. But, it can also be the day that begins your delivery from hell. Thankfully, that's what it was for me.

It was July 4, 1992. Earlier that day I walked down to the South Sea Seaport, where crowds of tourists milled about, jamming the streets and walkways. It was a beautiful day, and the harbor was full of boats and celebrations were in full swing. At first, I enjoyed he warmth of the sun on my face and the feeling of being out of the confines of my very dark and dismal East Village apartment. I wish I could say that I was unlike the other junkies who populated the run-down tenements in "Alphabet City," that I was of "special" circumstances. The truth, however, is that I was not. My apartment had the same darkened windows, the same torn and worn-out sofas, the same dirty bed linens, and the same filthy carpets as all the rest. I lived in the same ragged jeans and t-shirt for days on end, rarely bothering to wash myself, let alone my clothing. It is ironic that, after fighting for years to clean up Grey Gardens, here I was living in filth that even Edie and Mrs. Beale would have found unbearable. But for a few precious hours that day, I had escaped my self-constructed hell and was out in the sun and fresh air. It felt good … no, it felt wonderful. And then, it started. As the temperature rose, I began to sweat and before long it became unbearable. Then, my heart started racing and I knew that my body was beginning its craving. I made my way back to my dark and dirty apartment, and did what my body urged me to do. A few months before, during a particularly bad trip, I began to have thoughts of death. Now, they returned. I could see no way out except to die. My savings were gone. I was six months behind in my rent. I was alone. As I stood in my bathroom and looked at someone in the mirror who was literally unrecognizable to me, I was convinced that my last days of life were upon me. Suddenly, I was wracked with nausea. The sweat was pouring down me, and I began to retch and heave. My body was stressed beyond what seemed all human tolerance, and I was certain I was having a stroke or a heart attack. I turned on the faucet and began pouring cold water over me, but nothing would cool me down. I continued to dry heave for what seemed like an eternity, until, completely spent, I collapsed on the floor. I cried out from the pain. I cried out to God to please help me, to please "give me my life back."

I knew I was dying and that I needed to go to the hospital immediately. I crawled out of the bathroom, and, no longer having a telephone in my apartment (it had been shut off months earlier), I knew the only way was to get down onto the street where hopefully I could find someone to help me. I crawled on my hands and knees into the hallway of my building. No one was to be found. Somehow, I made it down the stairs and onto the street. I stood there, a truly pathetic soul and looked for help. The last thing I remember is collapsing on the sidewalk, which is where I was found by pedestrians. The paramedics were called and I was placed into an ambulance and transported to Cabrini Hospital. I vaguely remember the face of the EMT worker as he leaned over me in the ambulance. "I want my life back," I remember telling him before I passed out.

There in Cabrini Hospital, my desperate wish was granted. I was given an examination, diagnosed with several abscesses, severe dehydration, and a complete blockage in my left arm. I was also told, as I had long suspected, that I was HIV positive. By some miracle, despite the abuse I had inflicted upon my poor body, I had not developed AIDS. Ironically, I was so certain that my death was imminent from the drug abuse, the HIV diagnosis did not have the devastating effect on me that it probably would have had I been told years before. I was so relieved to be under medical care—in clean clothes, in a clean bed, with people watching over me—that the thought of what that diagnosis meant didn't even cross my mind. My prayer had been answered; I was given the opportunity to get my life back. However long that life would last was not my concern at the time. I was alive, and that was all that mattered.

After I was physically well enough to leave Cabrini Hospital, I checked into the Smithers Rehabilitation Center and slowly began to make my way back to the land of the living. I had thirty days of inpatient treatment in which I really began the hard work of recovery. In discussing my addictive behavior with the staff, the question that really hit it home for me was a simple one, yet it changed everything: "Do you realize the wreckage that you caused in your life, from everything you had to everything that you have lost?" *Everything that you have lost.* This was not a new thought to me, but it was the first time I truly considered the concept sober and the sheer weight of its reality brought me to my knees. Anyone one grappling with addiction will tell you that is the only place from where you can begin process of true recovery.

After my thirty days were up, I enrolled in an out-patient program that allowed me to be on my own and begin to rebuild my life. I had some major choices to make. It was clear to me that the people, places and things in my life had to be cleared completely from my life. This entire renovation was to be completed from top to bottom or nothing would work. My life in recovery would be lighter—less complex—and infinitely more manageable.

I slowly made the necessary changes. Addiction re-wires your personality; through the process of working the 12 steps, I was re-wiring myself back. Through a "fellow traveler," I found a part-time job at a taxi company as a driver, which was perfect for me. It allowed me the opportunity to make some money but also gave me the freedom to be able to go to meetings, call my sponsor, and do whatever necessary to continue to get better. Obviously, I could not return to my former apartment near Tompkins Square; not only was I virtually evicted from it, there was no way I could maintain my sobriety in the drug-infested area that was the East Village at the time. No, I needed to be as far away from that as I could get. Some wonderful and generous new friends allowed me the use of their sofas and spare bedrooms, but I knew I had to find my own place as soon as possible.

Before long, I heard of a small apartment in Queens that sounded perfect. It was quiet, private, and most importantly, I could afford it! As I looked around the neighborhood, I contemplated whether or not I could really live in Queens again—memories of my childhood lurked everywhere—and then I opened a door at the back of the unit and that settled the matter once and for all. There, before me, was a garden. A wonderful, private little patch of green space. After years of lovingly tending to soil that belonged to someone else, I finally had a patch of earth that would be mine, and mine alone. That was all I needed to see. I was home.

CHAPTER SEVEN:
ONCE MORE INTO THE GARDEN

The traffic careened about us as I made my way down 57th Street toward the East Side. It was the typical rush hour madness that I was familiar with from my years behind the wheel of a cab. But today, with my special fare, Albert Maysles, next to me in the front seat, I barely perceived it. How could so much have happened to all of us since we last saw each other? Thirty years' worth of life—and death—had gone by in the blink of an eye, it seemed. Mrs. Beale gone, Edie passed, and David gone as well. Only for some miracle and the grace of God was I still around, and so was my friend Albert. It felt so good to be alive.

And there was more on the horizon. Albert said that a musical was being written about our lives at Grey Gardens that was possibly headed to Broadway. There was also new documentary film that was to be culled from the hours of unused footage that Albert and David had shot all those years ago—a sort of sequel, if you will. And there was even talk of a new feature film in which actresses would portray Mrs. Beale and Edie. My mind raced with all these sudden prospects; after thirty years, *Grey Gardens* was suddenly reborn.

I had so many questions for Albert. Who could possibly play Mrs. Beale? Edie? I couldn't begin to imagine. Edie had once told me about a producer from Hollywood coming to the house years before and wanting to make a movie of her life starring actress Julie Christie. Edie turned him down flat. If anyone was going to portray Edith Beale, she said, it was going to be Edith Beale. And of course, with the Maysles film of *Grey Gardens*, that was exactly what happened. Albert said that he wasn't sure about the details of any of the projects, but that he was certain that the producers of the musical would want to talk with me now that I was "found." *Wait a minute*, I thought ... *talk with me?* "Do you mean that someone is going to play *me?*" I asked, more than a little anxious about the thought. He shrugged his shoulders and smiled ... filming me the entire time. We spent the rest of the afternoon rambling around midtown Manhattan, with me driving and talking and Albert filming. It was a wonderful reunion.

Finally, we said our goodbyes and Albert told me he'd be in touch in a few days. He would make arrangements for me to attend a rehearsal of the musical. I couldn't believe it. How was all this possible? I drove home to Queens with my mind reeling. After all these years, I would be "returning" to Grey Gardens.

Within a few days, it was all set up. The cast was performing a staged reading of the new musical at the Peter B. Lewis Theatre at the Guggenheim Museum later that week and I was invited. Despite my passion for art, I had never set foot in the Guggenheim before and now I was entering this iconic landmark to watch a play that was in part about my life! I was beside myself with anticipation ... and trepidation. I had no idea what to expect. Although it had been nearly thirty years and what felt like several lifetimes since I was with the Beales, I still remembered the feelings of anger and frustration I experienced that night in East Hampton when I first saw the film. Would this new play make me seem like the opportunist and manipulator that Edie's portrayed me as? It's a disturbing sensation to watch yourself being discussed behind your back in front of your face. Since Mrs. Beale died and I left East Hampton, I did my best to try and distance myself from "the Marble Faun." It wasn't difficult in places where the film had never been shown. And as the years passed and my resemblance to that young, scruffy boy in the *Newsday* sweatshirt grew less and less, the film itself became a dim and distant memory. Now, suddenly, it was all back and I had to ask myself: Had enough time passed that I would be able not only to confront my past again, but to embrace it?

The theatre was packed that afternoon as I took my seat. There was a lot of excited chatter going on about me, but none of it registered because I felt like I was existing in a dream. These people were just here to watch the reading of a new play, but I was about to see my life played out onstage. I could only imagine what Edie would say!

The house lights dimmed and the actors made their way onstage. It took some time for me to figure out just who was supposed to be playing whom. Since there were no costumes and the actors were simply in street clothes, it was a bit difficult to determine just what was going on. I had been told by Albert that the writers of the musical had structured the first act as a sort of fantasy about what life may have been like at Grey Gardens during its glory days, when Mr. and Mrs. Beale were still married and Edie was a young woman. It was wonderful to see the magnificent Christine Ebersole play Mrs. Beale with such elegance and style; it was exactly how I always imagined her to be in her younger days. I giggled to see the writer's ideas of people that I had heard so much about, such as Mrs. Beale's father and Gould. As the first act ended, a young Edie runs away from home to go to New York City, upset that her mother has ruined her engagement to Joe Kennedy, Jr., and Mrs. Beale is left alone. This was a bit of dramatic license on the writer's part; Edie was never engaged to Joe Kennedy Jr., although she told me that they had briefly dated. Moreover, she had received her mother's blessing to move to New York to pursue a theatrical career, she did not run away. Still, the play was dramatic and entertaining and I enjoyed it very much.

I was nervous at the break between acts, because I knew that I was about to see the writer's version of me. Finally, the audience took their seats and the lights in the theatre dimmed. As the second act began, Christine Ebersole made her way to center stage and into the same position that she was in at the end of Act One. Except that now, instead of playing Mrs. Beale, she was playing *Edie!* It was incredible. Her entire demeanor and physicality had changed, and she sounded and moved just like Edie. I was dumbfounded. The opening scene was basically the same scene in the movie when Edie first greets the Maysles and explains her "costume for the day" to them. In this show, however, she was greeting and explaining it to the audience—in a song! I laughed so hard at how perfectly it was realized. Edie would have been over the moon with happiness.

Then, the young and very good-looking actor named Matt Cavanaugh, who had played Joe Kennedy Jr., in the first act, came onstage in a dirty *Newsday* sweatshirt and jeans ... and my stomach felt like it dropped to my feet. *He was playing me!* To say that it was flattering to have this handsome young man portraying me is an understatement. He demonstrated a beautiful singing voice in the first act, so I was a little disappointed that as "Jerry" he had no songs in the second. But he did have a wonderful moment with Mrs. Beale, now played by actress Mary Louise Wilson, who sang a song to him called "Jerry Likes My Corn." I couldn't believe it! A song about our cooking ritual with corn on the cob! I was so moved. The song perfectly captured our special feelings for each other. I was so happy that my relationship with Mrs. Beale was honored in that way.

The second half of the musical was basically scenes from the film played out on stage but frequently in song. Of course, as in the film, there were the moments where Edie said negative things about me, but it didn't matter anymore. The true affection between Mrs. Beale and me was depicted so beautifully, and that was what was important. I knew that in heaven, both Edie and Mrs. Beale were smiling down and pleased with this version of our life. Both had always said that they wished that the film *Grey Gardens* had been a musical, and now it was.

When the play ended, the audience gathered at the foot of the stage and Matt Cavenaugh came toward me. I don't know who was more nervous at this meeting, Matt or me. He appeared calm, cool, and professional, but I was a wreck! "I guess you get to play me, you poor fellow," I said to him, attempting to break the ice. He laughed and told me how great it was to meet me. Next, I was introduced to the star, Christine Ebersol. "The *real* Jerry!" she exclaimed as she grasped my hand in a handshake. She was not only just as beautiful up close, she was kind and gracious. "Yes," I said to myself, "Edie would approve." Finally, there was Mary Louise Wilson, who played the elderly Mrs. Beale. Before the play, I think I was the more nervous about the prospect of seeing her performance than I was about seeing the actor who was to play me. I felt very protective of my beloved friend and wanted to be sure that she was portrayed accurately. I need not have worried. Mary Louise Wilson was a wonderful performer. She truly captured the humor and kind-heartedness of the woman

I knew, not to mention her incredible intelligence and feistiness. I told her how much I appreciated her sensitive and compassionate performance and she seemed very pleased, even giving me a little kiss on the cheek—just like Mrs. Beale used to do all those years ago.

A few days after attending the reading of the musical, I was invited by Albert to come to Maysles Films and watch some of the footage he was editing into the sequel to *Grey Gardens*. It had been many years since I had seen the original film. The last time was at a revival house in downtown Manhattan. I was driving down Houston Street when I spied something familiar on the sidewalk outside a small theatre; it was the original *Grey Gardens* poster advertising a showing of the film that week. I gathered together a small group of friends and attended a showing later that week. Remembering my reaction the first time I saw the film in East Hampton, I was worried about seeing it again—especially with friends who didn't know me as that scruffy, young boy. But after twenty-five years, the movie had little effect on me. In fact, it was as if I was watching someone else on that screen, so little did I recognize that timid teenager on the screen before me. I guess life and its inherent lessons had given me a new perspective and appreciation for it all.

I felt somewhat the same way as Albert showed me the footage he was putting into the new film, which was eventually to be called *The Beales of Grey Gardens*. It was exciting and emotionally stirring to see moments between Mrs. Beale and me that I had forgotten, and the affection that I felt for her washed over me again. But *who was* that kid in the dirty sweatshirt and shoulder length frizzy hair? I wanted to reach into the video monitor and shake him and tell him to stop and pay attention to what was happening in front of him. Life moves more swiftly than he can imagine. I wanted to tell him to pay attention to every detail; memorize every piece of furniture— every scent—every color—every feeling that he was experiencing back then since it would be gone before he knew it. I also wanted to advise that young pup not to get caught up in the petty details of life; what seems like life and death to you today, will turn out to be of little to no consequence tomorrow. But mostly, I wanted to see Mrs. Beale again, tell her how much she meant to me and how I have never forgotten the effect she had on my life and was still having to that day.

As with the original *Grey Gardens*, there was magic to the footage. Albert's camera is honest and nonjudgmental; there is no opinion about what is going on, the filming just *is*. I had forgotten so much of what he was showing me (how many of us remember things that happened over thirty years before?), and it affected me as if it were happening for the first time.

When the lights came back on, I sat for a few moments attempting to digest all I had just seen. To be able to see scenes in your life played out on a screen—so vivid and clear—how to describe it? I think it is the closest thing to time travel that a person can experience and the result is indescribable. As I sat there, unable to express how much this whole experience meant to me, Albert came over and sat next to me. He had a mischievous smile on his face that seemed to indicate that he had even more up his sleeve. Leave it to him to have a trump card. "How would you like to go back and visit Grey Gardens again?" he asked.

It had been nearly three decades since I set foot in that mansion, though many times over the years I made occasional visits to East Hampton. My friend Wayne lived in Sag Harbor, not far from East Hampton, as did a few other friends I had made over the years. But only he knew of my history with the Beales; I kept my Grey Gardens memories mostly to myself. I think it was because I was afraid of people reacting to me as the interloper and opportunist that Edie had tried to paint me as in the film. Or maybe it was because I simply wanted to keep my Grey Gardens memories private; somehow, they felt more special to me that way. Through the years, I would find myself absentmindedly driving in the direction of the mansion, wondering who owned it, what it might look like inside now that I'd heard it had been restored. I would park my car about five hundred feet away and take the slow walk down West End Road toward the house. I would stand outside the house and study it as I had in my teen years, but this time witnessing its slow rebirth and growth as the new owners pulled it back from the brink of decay and turned it into an elegant house once more.

While I was delighted that the home had been restored to its former glory, some changes puzzled me. What happened to the shutters? Who chose the pinkish-red color that now adorned the windows? Why a circular driveway that cut the spacious lawn in half? No matter. I was just happy that Mrs. Beale's beloved home was safe and secure. Often when I was in East Hampton, I would stop by Most Holy Trinity Cemetery to see Mrs. Beale and tell her of the changes that the house had undergone. How I wished that we could all have lived in the mansion as it was now, I told her. It was a beautiful place. She would have loved it so.

I can't say the same would have been true for Edie, however. I had heard, though I couldn't confirm it, that when she finally sold the home, she stipulated that no changes were to be made to the home whatsoever. A silly request to be sure, as who would spend so much money on the property only to leave it in its dangerous disrepair? Thankfully, this caveat was disregarded by the renowned *Washington Post* editor Ben Bradlee and his wife, Sally Quinn, and I imagine that they spent many millions to restore the home. I don't know for sure if it's a true story, but it certainly sounds like something Edie would have done.

Despite my familiarity with the exterior changes that the house had undergone, I had no idea what the interior now looked like, and I was anxious to get a look inside. So, it was arranged that I would travel to East Hampton along with Albert (and his camera crew, of course) in a few weeks. The current tenant was Frances Hayward, a friend of the Bradlees.

We agreed to travel out to East Hampton on a Sunday

afternoon when traffic would be the lightest, and our journey could be leisurely and carefree. As I made my way to Albert's house, I began to get very nervous. I was hoping that I wouldn't become too emotional when we finally arrived. Mostly, though, I was excited.

It was a lovely Sunday for a drive, and in no time at all the low-end storefronts and warehouses of Queens gave way to the rolling hills and lush greenery that lined the Southern State Parkway. Albert began to snooze in the passenger seat of my cab as I made my way to Montauk Highway and past the familiar names of my youth: Tuckahoe, Watermill, Bridgehampton, and finally East Hampton. As Albert slept, I stopped at a roadside fruit stand where I purchased some lovely flowers to give to our hostess, Frances Hayward, as well as some bananas to munch on for the rest of our journey. Before I knew it, I was turning down Apaquogue Road and approaching Lily Pond Lane ... only a few hundred yards from Grey Gardens.

Although it had only been a few years since I had driven past the house, I was overcome with emotion at my first sight of the glorious mansion. In a word, it was spectacular. The wild mass of untamed weeds and grasses that once choked the front yard—running rampant over the boundaries of the house—were tamed to a clipped manicure. During my years there, access to the main entrance of the house from the street was blocked by that abandoned car, which of course was no more. In fact, very little remained of the wild and untamed jungle that was once the front lawn. But I was cheered by the sight of the enormous elm tree, under which I often took afternoon naps, not only surviving but thriving. This evidence of the constancy of nature comforted me in these familiar yet strangely new surroundings.

It was an odd sensation to drive the cab up this new driveway and hear the crunching of the blue slate beneath its wheels. Albert had arranged for an additional film crew to record our return to the mansion, and they were already present when we arrived. I slowly stepped out of the cab and closed the door. With the film crew only feet away from me, I had an overwhelming sense of déjà vu as I stood on the driveway and looked at the house before me. It certainly felt like 1973 again, but of course it wasn't. Albert was beside me, but David, Edie, and Mrs. Beale were all gone. Try as I might, I couldn't shake the feeling of sadness over that thought. It was a bittersweet moment. While my mind told me that I was standing at Grey Gardens, my eyes told me otherwise. Its restoration was miraculous, and the home that stood before me was grander than I could have ever imagined. Still, I felt a sudden pang of pain inside me. Yes, it was beautiful now—but it was beautiful then, too. To me, it was more beautiful than anyone could have imagined.

Slowly, I made my way around the front of the house— the film crew following me the whole time, yet keeping a respectful distance so I could be alone with my thoughts and feelings. A flood of memories overwhelmed me as my eyes caught familiar sights. There was Edie's wall, as

I used to call it, which was actually a wall that separated the Beales' property from their neighbors, the Hills, and their garden ("That's the famous walled garden," Edie had mused to the Maysles camera thirty years earlier). I walked over to the side of the house and looked up at the center window, which was Edie and Mrs. Beales' bedroom. Many was the time that I would stand under this window and call up to Mrs. Beale when Edie had locked me out of the house. I chuckled to myself and suppressed the urge to call up once again; how would doing so look on film? Besides which, I knew there was no one to answer back, "Just a minute, Little Jerry ..." How I wished I had one more chance to call out to Mrs. Beale, to rush up the stairs, and give her a tender kiss on her cheek.

I began to make my way toward the back of the house, walking toward the kitchen porch where I sheepishly peered into the windows. At the side of the porch, the massive branches of privet that had once shielded the grounds from sunlight was cleared away and the lawn was lush and green. This area was where Edie discussed the possibility of a vegetable garden with Brooks, and he dismissed it as not practical due to the lack of sunlight. That was certainly not the case now. Over to the side of the backyard of the house was Edie's beloved sea of leaves, where she had positioned the "unseen chair" all those years before to escape her mother's gaze. Now in its place was a full-sized swimming pool. "How Edie would have loved that," I thought to myself. Edie Beale, the great dancer and swimmer.

Eventually we made our way to the front of the house again, where we were greeted by Frances Hayward. She gave us a warm welcome and made me feel comfortable right away. I offered my hand in friendship to her. I was so happy that someone so warm and friendly was taking care of the house now. I said to myself, "Mrs. Beale would approve." We made some small talk and I retrieved the flowers I had purchased and gave them to her. "How lovely," she said. "Let's put them in some water. I am sure you would like to come inside and look around." I didn't know how to respond, I was so choked up by the experience. I nodded quickly, and we turned to enter the house.

The first thing I saw was the bannister. My eyes instinctively went to it and followed the bannister up to the second floor. It was remarkable to see it look exactly as it had all those years ago, or rather how it must have looked when it was originally installed—clean and bright and immaculate. I wanted to run upstairs and open the door to the bedroom. Instead, I took a deep breath. "All in good time," I thought. "I am sure we'll make it up there." For now, I was content just taking it all in.

A rush of images flooded my mind. The chimney hearths in the library and its twin in the dining room— clean and shining and waiting for the glow of an autumn fire. The windows in the dining room—I could see out of them to the front lawn. In the library, a lush striped sofa placed in the exact spot of my old army cot and makeshift tent. Back then, I would pin one half of the tent to a bookshelf and the second to Gould's piano, which, of course, was long gone. (In the course of the afternoon, I discovered the fate of that piano; not long after purchasing the house, Mrs. Quinn rested her hand on the keyboard and the grand piano collapsed to the floor!) The library now had a wall of custom-made bookshelves, running floor to ceiling and across the expanse of the western wall.

Frances Hayward was a gracious host, and invited us to have a seat on the sofa while she fetched some refreshments for us. Oh, and was I hungry? Should we order some pizza? "That would be nice," I said. "Thank you." I laughed to myself, remembering the days in Mrs. Beale's bedroom when she refused to consider delivered pizza when there was *pâté* on crackers and vanilla ice cream to be had. Frances was such a gracious host, and I was doing my best to be a gracious guest, and participate in polite conversation, but on the inside, I was desperate to get up and explore the house. She must have sensed this, because after a few more moments of small talk, she leaned toward me and said, "Jerry, you must be dying to see the rest of the house." I confessed that, yes, I would very much appreciate the opportunity to explore. She smiled and waved her hand. "By all means, Jerry—please feel free to explore. We'll let you know when the food arrives."

I immediately set out for the dining room toward the butler's pantry to see if Buster's old haunt, the dumb waiter, was still in existence. I opened the door to peek inside and saw a simple closet. "Ah, Buster, old buddy," I said to myself, "your dumbwaiter is gone." I made my way into the kitchen, once the domain of Perfection, and in its place was a state-of-the-art industrial stove, just like ones used in restaurants. The entire kitchen was completely new; even the back stairway had been removed and built over. Looking around this new and unfamiliar space, I felt absolutely no connection to what that I had once known. It was a sad feeling. Time moves on. It's inevitable, although to be completely honest, not always preferable.

I made my way back to the front foyer and climbed the stairway to the second floor. I walked first inside the boy's bedroom, which was the room where I would dump bags of freshly caught porgies then stand back as dozens of feral cats greedily devoured them. Naturally, there was no hole in the ceiling—and the smell of porgies had long since evaporated into the air. I had difficulty getting myself to appreciate that this was indeed the same home that was raided by Suffolk County Health Department for being "uninhabitable"; it was completely and utterly un-recognizable as Grey Gardens to me. I truly felt as if I were in a strange home, with no connection to my past.

I explored more rooms, including a few that I had never been able to enter all those years before because their entrances were blocked by fallen beams, or the doors were too warped too open. They were all lovely and beautifully furnished, just as you would expect. Then I came upon the sunroom, or "Pink Room," where I had said my final goodbye to Mrs. Beale. I noted that the door to the outside porch, where she had loved to lounge and feel the warm summer sun on her legs, was replaced by a window, and the porch itself was gone as well. I admit to feeling a bit deflated at this point in my tour; there was literally nothing left of the home that I had known. But, there was still one room left to be seen ... the most important room of all.

The "Center Bedroom." It was where we lived our lives; where every meaningful conversation took place and so many encounters occurred. In this room, Mrs. Beale sang, Edie danced, and a lonely boy found a family to call his own. The last time I had been inside it, Mrs. Beale had bestowed her final benediction on the film and my responsibility to preserve it—and by extension, our life together. I wasn't sure if I could handle it if things inside the room had been altered too much. So many things had changed since the last time I had opened this door; not just in the house but in life itself. Hesitantly, I turned the knob and slowly opened the door.

I was overjoyed. It looked exactly the same! Of course, it had been re-painted and re-decorated and removed of all traces of cats and raccoons. But essentially, it was the same. There were two twin beds in precisely the same location. A small table in between them. A dresser in the corner. I could hear the old sounds of arguments, singing, and endless banter between the Beales. As the bright sunlight came streaming through the light chiffon drapes I slowly made my way to the foot of the bed next to the door and sat at the very edge. It was where Mrs. Beale had been, and from this position she and I would discuss anything that came to mind. It was here that she would hand me a steaming hot cob of corn—lightly salted and smeared with gobs of butter—that she had prepared just for me. She would sing to me and tell the stories of her life. Sometimes Edie would come in and join us, frequently dance about in her corner of the room and, on occasion, goad me into joining her. Even with the freshly-painted walls and the crisp, new linens on the beds, this room—more than any other room I had entered—*felt the same.* In a strange way, it was if time had stopped. I took a few deep breaths. (I laughed at the thought that I *could* take a deep breath now, with all the cats gone.) I was on the brink of breaking down, and I desperately wanted to hold it together ... especially with Albert and Mrs. Hayward downstairs.

For just a brief moment, though, I let myself go. I allowed myself to feel the loss that I had been running from as long as I could remember. Not just the loss of Mrs. Beale and Edie, but the loss of Robert, the loss of countless friends, the loss of my mother, the loss of my family, and most importantly, the loss of that little boy from Brooklyn who wanted nothing but to be held and comforted and told that he was loved and safe. For many years, this strange and extraordinary place called Grey Gardens provided me with all that and more. It was filled with my family. Mrs. Beale, Edie, and I were, in those early years, the strongest and closest family imaginable and this was where we lived. To outsiders, it was a run down, filthy horror of a house, but to me it was paradise. Grey Gardens was my own, special Garden of Eden. It was my shelter. It was my protection. It was my home.

I sat for a few moments more before I heard the voices from downstairs calling out to me that the pizza had arrived. I was suddenly very hungry. I realized that I hadn't eaten anything all day but that banana at the fruit stand. Suddenly, I heard Mrs. Beale's voice—the first words she ever said to me—echoing in my mind: "You need to eat a boiled potato, chicken breast, and a green salad to keep that beautiful face."

I slowly got up off the bed.

"Would you like some corn, Jerry? He always compliments me on the way I do my corn."

I laughed and walked toward the door.

"You're Aquarius, aren't you, Jerry? That's what I saw when I first met you.'"

I stopped at the door and looked back into the room one last time.

"Well, for goodness sake ... the 'Marble Faun' is here."

I walked out and closed the door quietly behind me.

I am, Edie. I am.

ACKNOWLEDGMENTS

Jerry Torre

For the foundation of my life, virtues that were taught me that guide me to this very day, my mother, Helen Torre, and my father, Anthony Torre.

For inviting me to complete my high school years, with lifelong admiration, the Kalbacker family.

For the memory of my brother Robert Torre, a life here too brief and one that is forever in the Kingdom of Heaven.

For the love they shared and for being invited into their lives, Mrs. Edith Bouvier Beale and her devoted daughter, Miss Edie Beale. They will always be a part of my life.

For the genuine love taught to me by those who cared for me, it is my duty to continue to honor

Albert and David Maysles and their tireless work in the rarest of seasons at Grey Gardens.

For his kindness and his gentle soul, my dearest friend, Mr. Wayne Clinton Graves.

For his determination in this work, Tony Maietta, a dear friend since day one.

For his abounding consideration, deep friendship, and love, Ted Sheppard, who entered my life and become a lifelong confidant and family.

For all these people, my deepest and most sincere thanks and appreciation.

In addition, much respect and gratitude for all those who influenced my passion in the arts:

Wayland Flowers and Madame, Lynn Carter and company, Mrs. Jacqueline Kennedy Onassis, Mr. Aristotle Onassis, Jackie Klempay, Julie Wilson, and Chiam Gross.

And finally, to all the "Grey Gardeners"—a family of many who have been drawn to share the cornerstone of my life.

"You're in this world, you know."—Mrs. Edith Beale

Tony Maietta

Many years ago, I was killing time in my local video store looking for something unusual and engrossing to watch when the clerk asked me if I had ever seen the film *Grey Gardens*. When I confessed that I had not, he quickly ran to the shelf and placed a copy of the DVD in my hands and said to me, "Once you meet Edie Beale, your life will never be the same."

Truer words were never spoken.

Since that time, my obsession with all things *Grey Gardens* has never waned, and the opportunity to work with Jerry Torre in telling of his adventures with those two remarkable women is something for which I will always be grateful. So, first and foremost, I want to thank Jerry Torre for his willingness to share his life's adventures and for agreeing to go on this journey with me. It has been a long, and sometimes daunting prospect to capture the most ephemeral of entities—memory—and translate it into something tangible and lasting. My hope is that you are pleased with the results.

I must also thank Michael Compton for his unending support, friendship, and—when needed—legal expertise. In a very real sense, this book could never have been completed without your support and guidance, and I am forever grateful.

Thanks also to Ted Sheppard, for his calm and steady hand in a sometimes-stormy sea; Lawrence Helman, for his generosity and assistance in helping us find a home for this book; and Don Weise for seeing this book to its publication.

Huge thanks to the Maysles Institute, and especially to the late Albert Maysles, not only for writing the introduction to this book, but for the vision he and his brother had in bringing those two most unforgettable characters, Mrs. Edith Beale and her daughter, Edie, to the world. Without the Maysles, there would be no *Grey Gardens*; and my life—and the lives of millions of people around the world—would be much less interesting without it.

So many people provided support to me throughout the course of this journey, including, but not limited to: Marc Abbondanza, Stephen Dolginoff, Stan Bochniak, Michael Owens, Steven MacNicoll, Lawrence Zarian, John Samuels, Thomas J. Watson, Jeffrey Porterfield, and Scott Mauro.

Finally, but most importantly, thank you to my mother and father, Anthony and Jane Maietta. Your love and support of me not only in this venture, but throughout a lifetime of hopes, dreams and desires has been always been unwavering, unconditional, and unending. I love you with all my heart.

(Michael Bryant)

JERRY TORRE

Jerry Torre grew up in Brooklyn, New York and left home at age sixteen. Not long after leaving home, while working as an assistant gardener in East Hampton, New York he quite literally stumbled into the house and world known as Grey Gardens. Today, he lives happily with his partner, Ted, in New York City, dividing his time between his passion for sculpting, and in being a caretaker yet again for Grey Gardens—this time for its legacy. Jerry's website is jerrythemarblefaun.com.

(David Bryant)

TONY MAIETTA

Tony Maietta is a noted film and television historian, author and host. His work as a film historian and host includes numerous DVD documentaries and commentaries including the Emmy-nominated TCM series "Moguls and Movie Stars" (2010). As a writer and host he appeared in his own series *Here's Hollywood* (2012) as well as the CBS Home Video releases of *The Lucy Show* and *I Love Lucy*. For more information, visit his website: tony-maietta.com.

9 780999 517703